GIVEN TIME TO SAY GOODBYE

GIVEN TIME TO SAY GOODBYE

Dianne Leutner

ISBN: 0993434703
ISBN 13: 978-0-9934347-0-9
Library of Congress Control Number: 2015910933
Published by Three Boys Publishing
Produced and printed by Create Space, North Charleston, South Carolina

Acknowledgements

My siblings Peter, Ans, Christian and Toon Bressers. We shared this journey and didn't we do well? You are all so special in your own unique and special way. Peter for always being organised and helpful and taking on the role of eldest responsible sibling. Ans for being my amazing and sensible big sister. You are the one and only! Christian for always keeping the humour alive in all emotions. Toon, you are a male version of me and I totally get you!

Thank you to my proof readers. It was hard to let go of my baby. You made me believe in my book. Caroline Gilson for reading it in a day and enjoying it immensely. Karine Brissy-Hayes who had to go through a similar journey when her husband had terminal cancer and who truly believes the book will help people cope with cancer. Nicola Easton who told me that the book helped her grief her mother ten years on. I'm sorry it made you cry on the train all the time! Dr Bart Blaauw who tells me "It's a beautiful example of how you can prepare yourself to a healthy grieving process which is undeniably on its way."

Thank you in particular to my proof readers who went beyond the call of duty. Andrew Clover for analysing the book with graceful words, "Honouring your mother and father is a key component of health and happiness." Rebecca Smith, who helped me with the "English flow" as only a true English Rose can.

UK Literary Agent, Jonathan Lloyd of Curtis Brown, who gave me the most wonderful rejection letter I could have wished for in which he gave me the confidence to go ahead with self- publishing my work. You made me believe in my project by telling me that the writing is strong and incredibly moving on a poignant and important subject. Thank you for taking the time to give me the benefit of the doubt and liking my story.

Thank you to my friends, my angels, who were there on my journey with me and helped me to fly when my wings were broken.

Maggie and Liz for being there for part of my journey. I am so sad we had no time to say goodbye. I remember you both with love in my heart.

My three beautiful boys Luke, Henry and Rufus who make me realise every day, how delicately vulnerable life is. You make me want to make the most of the moments that the days have on offer.

Thank you to my husband Pete. Your strength and calm determination is exemplary. Thank you for holding my hand and for being my best friend.

I dedicate this book to my parents
Toon and Toos Bressers

You were two in a million
Thank you for unconditional love

Contents

Introduction

According to some philosophies, our lives move in seven-year cycles. My journey through the past seven years was intense, but it was also a journey during which I have experienced immense personal growth. During this period, I lost my father to bowel cancer, and I gave birth to a son at the age of forty-three, followed closely by losing my husband's twin sisters, age fifty, who died suddenly within six weeks of each other. A year after their passing, my father-in-law also died unexpectedly. Nine months later, my mother was diagnosed with terminal pancreatic cancer. It was yet another emotional and life-changing journey that was sealed with death.

I spent three years writing this book and shed many tears in the process. It will most probably make you cry, too; I would certainly not call it an easy read. I take you through the dark tunnel of my grieving journey, where you will learn that in the deepest darkness, the light is born. Grief needs to be felt and experienced. During my process, I realised that sometimes a tiny glimmer of light had more meaning than a thousand suns. I learned that light was born in silence and that I had to go to the depth of my soul to make the transformation into the light. I sincerely hope you will allow me to share with you the transformation that takes place at the end of the book.

When my parents were diagnosed with cancer, they were both in their mid- to late seventies, and in both cases it was classified as terminal from the start. The news from their oncologists was somber: "The cancer will win! Sooner rather than later." Their harsh words took away all hope of their getting better. The outlook for their future was bleak. The only certainty was a short remaining life followed by death. Everybody deals with terminal illness in their own way, be it by denial or perhaps by throwing the Bible against the wall. Although my parents' journey wasn't easy, they both did their best to embrace the big, dark cloud that is cancer and to face death in a courageous and positive way. Of course there were tears, fears, pain, and some periods of denial, but by facing up against this demon, a transformation took place, and a silver lining appeared—acceptance and recognition of love. Our journey became filled with hope, light, and positive energy, and as a result, it became a meaningful time during which my family grew stronger as a unit. It also made us grow substantially as individuals. My parents gave me life, but they also gave me the tools to deal with death and showed me that it isn't something to be scared of.

Dying is inevitable. Being in their seventies, my parents had been blessed with reasonably long and healthy lives, so accepting their fate must have been much easier for them than if they had been young. When they got diagnosed with terminal cancer, they chose to make this final part of their journey with their loved ones meaningful and fulfilling.

Around the time of my parents' death, my husband's sisters and father also died. It felt like a raging storm had hit, causing sudden and unreasonable destruction. Amid this storm was the birth of our son. This gave us a focus that pulled us through our sudden grief.

We all deal with loss in our own unique way. Every death is different. We are all unique as individuals, so we all grieve differently. I believe that if you embrace any living moment, be it a joyous or sad one, there is a gift in it. Only by being in the now will you find your true strengths. Try not to prefer one over the other, as there is great possibility for growth, love, and true wonder in all emotions.

1

My Childhood

I'm the middle of five children, nicely cushioned by siblings, all growing up in the '60s and '70s on a Dutch farm with playground among playground of Dutch countryside. I remember bringing in the cows from the field for milking and building huts and swings out of hay bales while my father milked the cows. It wasn't always play though, and every one of us children had to help out on the farm doing chores.

My mum and dad were of a generation in which cuddles and declarations of "I love you" were quite scarce, but I felt secure and loved and was a happy-go-lucky child. They made me into the confident person I am today. My parents were both from Catholic stock and were one of ten siblings each, so there were plenty of cousins who lived in the surrounding villages to play with during the weekends. Every Sunday, we would meet at my grandparents' house. The dads went off to play pool, the mums would chat, and the cousins would all play together in a safe and loving countryside environment.

Although life was happy and secure, it certainly wasn't without tragedy. Three cousins died in tragic accidents that affected me deeply. The death that affected me most happened when I was eleven. My twelve-year-old cousin, whom I was close to, had a tragic accident. She jumped off a cupboard onto her bed and fell, hitting the back of her neck on the bed rail. The Doctor told my uncle and aunt to put her to bed for some sleep, where she died only hours later. The smell of freesias still reminds me of that moment when I saw her lying in her coffin. I stood there in disbelief, looking at her lying there totally lifeless and still. It was the first time I had seen a dead body, and it was a life-changing experience. Writing about it now gives me shivers.

Just a few years after my cousin's tragic death, my eleven-year-old neighbor fell off her horse and died of severe head injuries a few days later, when the life-support machines were turned off. My mum was a close friend of the girl's mother, who had been widowed only two years earlier. My mum was there with her when they turned off the support machine. The brain damage was too severe, and there was no hope. I will never forget the howling sounds that came out of my parents' bedroom that following night. My mother, a calm person who would never shout at us, had to release her pain and disbelief. So many young lives were being lost around us; it was incomprehensible.

These tragic accidents were hard to understand. When I was a young teenager, I went through a stage of real fear and depression. I realised at an early age how fragile life was. For at least a year, around the age of thirteen, I was living in a little bubble surrounded by fear. I felt detached from reality for a while, and anxious thoughts were taking a grip on my life. My life was filled with fear of death, war, and of the end of the world. I believe now that the loss of these young lives deeply affected my moods at that time.

My late teens were filled with good times. I had a solid boyfriend, many good friends, and a pretty cool life. My parents were strict about certain things but gave me a lot of freedom on my journey to self-discovery and encouraged independence.

When I was twenty, I met Pete, a man from England. I fell in love with his calming patience, perseverance, and the best forearms I had ever set eyes on and followed my heart to be with him in England at the young age of only twenty-one. We married ten years later in the hope that we would have a family of our own. We are blessed with three sons: Luke, Henry, and Rufus. When I followed my heart and took all my belongings to England to live with Pete, leaving my happy life in Holland, and travelled across the sea with him, I didn't realise that leaving my home and family might become a point of conflict in the future.

2

Dad's Journey

Being the youngest girl in the family, I was very much a daddy's girl in his eyes, but also in the eyes of my siblings. I could do no wrong! Our relationship was straightforward and uncomplicated, and we had an understanding. Perhaps I took a little advantage of my position sometimes, but I would make sure it would be subtle. He always told me I was the easiest child as long as I got my own way. He didn't even attempt to stop me at the young age of twenty-one, when I followed my heart to England to be with the man I fell in love with. He knew only too well that trying to stop his little girl would be a losing battle. He supported me financially and emotionally all the way.

It was only months after I turned forty when my world was rocked, and I felt broken. He is not part of my physical world now, but I feel his light shining on me and working within me through his sayings and beliefs that are engraved in my heart. To this day, they are making me strong and loving. This is how our journey started soon after my fortieth birthday.

MAY 16, 2006 – FAMILY VISIT

My precious dad and his two brothers, my hilariously funny uncles, were accompanying me on the ferry on my way back from my native Holland to England, where my excited seven- and four-year-old sons, and my husband were awaiting me at home. As the familiar Dover Cliffs came into sight, I was observing my father and his only two surviving siblings out of a family of ten. I was sitting with my book in a row of seats behind them. I wanted them to have a special time on their miniholiday together.

I was enjoying a wonderful view of the back of my father, with his brothers sitting on either side in silhouette as the early evening sun came beaming in through the ship window from the west. Beyond the silhouette of the threesome lay the white Cliffs of Dover in the beautiful land called Kent, which I had been calling my adopted home for nearly twenty years. The three brothers were excited, and my father was proud to show them the country that his daughter had moved to. It tickled me to see him at seventy-six with his two older brothers in this unusual situ. I could imagine them as three little boys all those years ago. There was a real sense of love and playfulness among them that was touching.

It was a wonderful homecoming, and it felt great to see my little boys and my husband. I had been away for only one night and found it hard to leave them for even such a short period of time. When I am separated from my children, there is always a real personal fear and anxiety that something terrible might happen to them while I'm not there. I have always wondered if these intrusive thoughts have something to do with my karma or if it is because of all the sad losses I had to experience as a child. Anyway, it felt good to have all of us together in the house.

During the few days that followed, I took my dad and uncles to some special places, and the conversation, although always filled with lots of humour, was often philosophical and spiritual. One day, I was sitting on a bench with the three of them outside Canterbury Cathedral, where a funeral was taking place. We watched the coffin being carried into the prestigious cathedral and were wondering which "well to do" person was in there. It didn't take long for the conversation to turn to their own deaths and funerals. They were jokingly guessing which of the three of them would die next. They all thought that, because my father was the youngest and most fit, he would almost definitely go last. We can all guess, but nobody knows what lies ahead.

2–13 AUGUST 2006
SUMMER BREAK

When we got home to Holland for our summer break, I was concerned to find my father not too well. He had troubles sleeping, which was extremely unusual for him and worrying for us. When I was a little girl, the sound of him snoring had given me a sense of comfort that all was well in the house but that feeling of all being well wasn't there that summer. He experienced extreme pain while lying down, which made it very difficult to sleep. This made him feel exhausted during the day. He really wasn't himself, but visits to the doctor hadn't come up with anything particular or worrying. We thought it might just be the heat wave that was making him suffer.

I was relieved that we would be going on a little camping trip with my sister and her children, so we weren't going to create extra work for my mother. We would go back after our camping trip to stay with them for the last few days of our visit.

My sister didn't seem too concerned, so I thought things would probably turn out OK. I figured it was just a short-lived problem that would fix itself in time, like most ailments generally do. We enjoyed our camping holiday and tried not to worry about it.

On our return to my parents' house a week later, things hadn't improved. My father would be up all night, and it was starting to also take its toll on my mother, who was now giving him Reiki healing for a large part of the night to help him have some relaxation and sleep. They were both exhausted. Blood test results came back with no conclusion. They kept struggling on and were hoping that things would soon settle down. We were suspecting all sorts of things that it could be, such as nerve pain, kidney stones, fluid on the heart and lungs, complications with his diabetes, but certainly not cancer. The blood test told us that everything looked clear on that front, and after all, we weren't the kind of family that would be struck by cancer!

SUNDAY, AUGUST 13
CYCLING ALONG

On Sunday afternoon, we were to depart for England again. The whole family met at my parent's house, like we did every Sunday morning. It was a beautiful, sunny day, and we all sat in the garden, chatting. The grandchildren were climbing trees and jumping on the trampoline, and my mother was carrying trays in and out of the kitchen with coffee and yummy cakes. I could tell that my father was struggling with all the visitors, even though they were his own children and grandchildren. He decided to go on a little bike ride for some peace and quiet; cycling was something he was still able to do. I decided that I wanted to join him, and he seemed to like the idea. We were quietly cycling next to each other on a familiar path through the woods that surround the village. I felt sad as I watched him slowly cycling along, in deep thought with his head slightly bent down. He looked so frail and vulnerable, not at all like my strong dad who, only weeks earlier, was still swimming and walking on a daily basis, something he had done all his life, with a huge smile on his face. That posture of happiness and strength had disappeared behind a huge, dark cloud of uncertainty, tiredness, and pain. My eyes took me to the hands that had provided for me all my life and that were now holding the handlebars of his bicycle tightly. I realised that he had changed into a shaky old man, barely able to fulfill his passion of taking a simple cycle ride around the village. I was quietly crying. I wiped away the tears that were rolling down my cheeks while cycling behind him slightly so he couldn't see me upset. I felt devastated by the thought that this could be our last-ever cycle ride together. I was realising there and then that he was really unwell. I despised the thought of having to go back to England and leave my sick father behind.

Later that afternoon, when the time came to say goodbye, I held myself together when I kissed him but cried all the way back home. I was particularly upset when reaching the Cliffs of Dover, thinking about the time only a few months earlier when my father was in such good spirits when he reached the English shores with his beloved brothers. I had a feeling from deep down inside me that that trip we had taken in May would become my father's last visit to England.

AUGUST 14–SEPTEMBER 13
STILL NO ANSWERS

My father had to suffer another month of sleepless nights. He couldn't lie in bed, and the only sleep he occasionally got was sitting upright in his chair. The pain was increasing on a daily basis, but still there was no medical explanation. He didn't enjoy eating and was losing weight extremely fast. He devoted the little bit of energy he had left to trying to cope with the pain. Both my parents were in a terrible state of desperation. Their lives had become intolerable. Not knowing what was wrong for so long with this extreme suffering was cruel; you wouldn't even let your pet go through it. Everybody in the family felt helpless. We all desperately needed somebody to tell us where to go next. We needed a third party to take control of the situation. We were stagnated in a cycle of pain, and we didn't know the way out. My father had been to the hospital to see several specialists, but still there were no answers.

My sister told me that after one of his short spells of sleep, my dad told her that he had had a nightmare in which he was confronted by a big, black snake. The dream had terrified him, but he told her that despite his fear, he managed to bite the snake's head off.

SEPTEMBER 14
APPOINTMENT

We were all desperately trying to make things more comfortable for him. My sister would meditate with him and do visualizations with him travelling to the region of pain. Together they would try and transform this pain, but nothing really helped or gave him any comfort. My father decided to go and see the osteopath again; he was a family friend. My dad had seen him before, earlier on in the progression of pain, and usually he felt a little relief after his visits with him. The osteopath sensed that something was very wrong and told my dad to go back to hospital and demand a scan as soon as possible.

My brother rang the hospital and again expressed our extreme concern. We were all relieved when the hospital offered an appointment soon. My father was finally booked for an MRI scan early the next morning.

SEPTEMBER 15
DIAGNOSIS

It was the day of the scan, and I was relieved and nervous at the same time. I was dreading the outcome but couldn't wait to finally find out the cause of my dad's extreme pain. His suffering of the last six weeks or so was inhumane and cruel.

At 2:30 p.m. in the afternoon, the phone rang, and I knew from looking at the number that it was my sister. It was the call and the very news I had been dreading. I picked up the phone in a sort of trance. I knew I would have to just go with the flow and deal with whatever the news would be.

My sister gave me the news straight away: "Dad has cancer, and it doesn't look good." I felt battered, I felt hurt, I felt emotions I couldn't describe—intense feelings that were unknown to me. There had been too many bad days, and I felt that the world was against us. No gift was to be found on that day. I had only seen cancer from a distance in other families, and it always looked scary. The realisation that I could lose my father to cancer soon kicked in. I had always presumed that my father would die of a heart attack like his brothers and his father. That was something I had prepared myself for, but I really wasn't prepared for cancer. The awful disease that everybody is scared of had hit my family. It had struck my beloved father, and the journey that lay ahead was unknown and petrifying. I felt like somebody had thrown me into a dark valley with very little light.

SEPTEMBER 18, 2006
THREE DAYS AFTER THE DIAGNOSIS

Two days on, the valley didn't look quite so dark. My father had been given very strong pain medication and was now practically pain-free. He went from an excruciating, unbearable state of pain to feeling normal, and that was a major accomplishment. The whole family was feeling relief that he was finally cured of this cruel pain. Instead of anticipating what could be wrong in a state of great emotional and physical hurt and uncertainty, we were now dealing with something that was real, concrete, set in stone. My father had cancer. We finally knew what was wrong with him, and we were dealing with it. He was not in pain, and for now, after months of suffering, being comfortable was the most amazing gift. Dark thoughts of having to live with that discomfort and anguish for the rest of his life must have crossed his mind. The contrast of how he felt physically only days earlier was life changing for him and for us as a family. Dealing with the cancer would be the next step, but for now he enjoyed the immense relief and the quality of life that this ease had brought.

My family decided to start a Weblog to inform family and friends of his journey and also to avoid exessive phone calls. We all contributed to it on different significant days.

Weblog: Monday, September 18–Peter

The fluid going into him has been reduced from 2 liters to 0.5 liter per day. The morphine is also being reduced on a daily basis. Small amounts of food and catching up on sleep have resulted in a less tired father. He enjoys some TV and even asked for the newspaper today, showing that he is still concerned about the happenings in the world.

A sample of his lymph nodes has been taken, and a colonoscopy has been planned for Thursday. We are hoping for more news at the beginning of next week.

Weblog: Wednesday, September 20–Christian

Visited Dad this evening. When I walked in at seven o clock, he said, "Come on, Christian. Let's go for a walk around the wards." I thought that was a good sign.
A meeting with the oncologist is planned for Monday, so we have a little while to wait until we receive the result. Toon sends his regards to all the followers on this blog.

Weblog: Thursday, September 21–Peter

The news from the doctor after the colonoscopy was not good. Cancer has been diagnosed in the first part of the large intestine and has spread to the lymph nodes around that area. On the CT scan, they have also noticed dark patches on the liver. They are not sure if these patches are innocent cysts or cancer yet. The size of the tumor was too large for the endoscopy to pass it. The advice of the doctors is to operate, remove as much of the tumor as possible, and try to prevent the large intestine from becoming totally blocked. The chances of completely removing the tumour are very slim. It was advised to talk about possible treatments after the operation.

Toon and his family have decided to go ahead with the operation, which is expected to take place within two weeks. The surgeon will talk to him tomorrow. Toon is awaiting a relatively common operation that doesn't carry too many risks. Luckily, he is a very fit man who was doing two hours of exercise per day until only a few months ago, which means he should recover well after the operation. We should have a much clearer idea of the situation after the operation.

SEPTEMBER 21
SIX DAYS AFTER THE DIAGNOSIS

These were difficult times for me. All of this was happening in Holland, and I couldn't be there to support my parents and siblings. I cried a lot during this period. There was hope, of course, but I prepared myself for the worst--case scenario. It was looking likely that he would die from the cancer, but how and when were questions I was asking myself. I felt that I was already grieving for my father before I even knew that his cancer was terminal. I took myself for long walks through the glorious English countryside and would sit, reflect, and allow myself to just be. This "being" would enable me to release my emotions. I cried many tears while being at one with nature. September 2006 was beautiful. Those walks in late summer sunshine with times built in for reflection turned out to be therapeutic. I analyzed my relationship with my father and the things we had shared in life. Our bond and love for each other was pure and solid, and I didn't feel that any healing needed to take place between us. We had no unresolved issues—just loving until the day he died, whenever that day would be. The realisation of this gave me inner peace and made me realise that whatever time was left had the potential of being quality time.

Weblog: Friday, September 22–Ans

Dad appeared well when we visited him today. He told us about the meeting he had with the surgeon, which has given him peace of mind, clarity, and something to hold onto. We hope the operation will take place soon, although a date and time hasn't yet been given. Dad is so very touched by all your cards and messages of good and positive thoughts. He is grateful for all the people who are caring for him but also those thinking of him. I know many of you have asked to visit, which is really touching, but Toon is not up to visitors outside his closest family just yet. For our mother, the past few months have been mentally and physically exhausting, and she is also very tired. If you want to call, please call one of the children.

Weblog: Saturday, September 23–Peter

Dad appears well today. He has had a good night's sleep and has enjoyed his food. The drip has been taken off, and the pain medication has been reduced to twice per day.

Weblog: Sunday, September 24–Christian

Dad has been in hospital for a week now and took a walk outside for the first time in seven days. The weather was lovely, and we thought it was about time for him to breathe in some fresh air, together with his son, daughter-in-law and grandchildren. It did him a world of good. Still no news about when the operation will take place. Hoping for a date tomorrow.

It must have been tough knowing that the cancer was still growing inside him. I had so much respect for his patience about when the operation would take place. I think if it were me, I would just want to have it out now! All he could do was go with the flow and get strong in preparation for the big day. In the meantime, he was enjoying some intense quality time with the family.

Dad's operation will take place on Wednesday. We are all pleased that it will be sooner rather than later.

Dad went home for the afternoon today. At two o'clock, we drove him home, where his good friend was awaiting him. It was an emotional afternoon with mixed feelings. Of course, there's no place like home, and he really enjoyed walking through his garden. The most disturbing thing about being home was seeing his armchair, where he experienced two months of pain and sleepless nights. For now, he was relieved of his pain, and he didn't want to revisit the awful time spent in that chair, which felt still so raw. The anxiety about the operation and the uncertainty of the near future were also playing on his mind, in contrast with the happy memories of good health that he had spent in his house. He was glad to slip back into his hospital bed in the early hours of the evening after an emotional day.

Tomorrow he will start preparing for the operation and transfer to the surgical ward. His intestines will have to be cleansed, which means no food and laxatives. All in all, an unpleasant and busy day lies ahead.

Now that I knew when the operation would take place, I could plan my next trip to Holland. I had never left my children for longer than one day and found it hard to leave them, but I knew I had no real choice in the matter. I would have to leave them in England so I could give my parents all the love and attention they needed. Because I had to work around my husband's work schedule, I decided I would go after Dad's operation had taken place. I knew my dad would be excited to see me, and once the anxiety of the operation was behind him, it was something to look forward to for both of us.

Weblog: Tuesday, September 26–Christian

We have the latest news from the hospital. The countdown has begun—the operation will be at 11:00 a.m. and is expected to last about one and a half hours. So that means that in twenty-four hours' time, the operation will be behind us. Dad is ready for it. The surgeon visited him this afternoon and sat on the edge of the bed with him, explaining once more the procedure and the potential outcomes of the operation. There seemed to be a nice click between Dad and the surgeon, who told Dad, "Mr. Bressers, you look very good for your age." Of course that cheered him up and was a good compliment coming from the doctor. One more night, and hopefully we can start on our road to recovery.

Weblog: Tuesday, September 26–Ans

Dad seemed introverted today, which seems logical seeing that he has such a big operation ahead of him. Also, the moment of truth has come.

Many friends and family are burning candles for him. For us children, it feels comforting to have so much love and support out there. What an amazing medium the Internet can be. Just out of nowhere, a network of connection and support has emerged.

I was grateful to be there when Dad moved to the surgical ward this afternoon. His bed, together with his cards, pictures, and chocolates have moved to ward number B1. He is in a room with one other person, and he is expected to be there for a while after the operation. Mum will visit him tonight, and after that it, will be a waiting game until after the operation.

An anxious night and morning followed for all of us. There are dangers attached to such a complex operation. Also, there is the anxiety about the outcome. So many uncertainties—they made my night a restless one.

Weblog: September 27–Christian and Peter

Dad got operated on around midday. A meeting with the surgeon was scheduled after the operation at six o'clock. Dad had recovered from the anesthetic and had woken up with high hopes. He told us, "I hope they got rid of most of the tumor." He was feeling relatively OK and didn't have any pain. Just high hopes!

However…the surgeon came with bad news. He told us that the tumor had grown too large to be removed, and Dad won't be able to be cured. During the operation, a bypass was made where the small intestine got connected to a healthy part of the large intestine. The cancer that affected part of the large intestine was now no longer part of the digestive system, and this should prevent further blockages. The message from the surgeon was devastating. We all had hoped and prayed for a better outcome.

This was yet another huge chunk of bad news. The cancer was terminal. We would lose him sooner rather than later. How could I possibly face him the next day, knowing that he was now officially dying of cancer?

Weblog: Thursday, September 28–Toos, my mother
Day after the operation

I woke up early and sensed that something was wrong. I rang the hospital at eight o'clock, and my feelings were confirmed. Toon was in a lot of pain and had an emergency operation. Something had gone wrong internally and needed adjusting.

When I visited him later this afternoon, I was relieved to see him with a smile on his face again. We do not have a choice in how the terminal illness is going to take shape, but we have a choice in making the most of what we have left. I am prepared for the suffering; we have already done quite of lot of that in the past few months. Misery is optional. Life has many adversities, and there is no doubt that Toon's illness is one of them, but we are determined to not let this control the opportunities for happiness that we have left in our lives.

The sun rises in the same place as it sets
Like the sun never really sets,
the journey of our souls never really ends.

SEPTEMBER 28
FACING MY DYING FATHER
Unaware of what was happening to my dad in the operating theatre, I travelled to Brussels by train early that morning.

The person sitting next to me on the train was reading *The Power of Now* by Eckhart Tolle. The book teaches people about the importance of living in the present. *How appropriate*, I thought, as I realised that the power of now was so relevant in my situation. The fact that this man was reading that particular book was a sign for me that made me realise the need to treasure every moment I had left with my father.

My youngest brother, Toon Jr., was to meet me at a tiny Belgian train station. I had changed trains in Brussels. When he met me at the station, he seemed very together and relatively optimistic. He lived walking distance away from my parents and had been there in person with them ever since my father had fallen ill. I felt as if I had been an outsider far away in England, with just a telephone connection. I was now just about to join this journey that perhaps seemed worse on the outside than it actually was on the inside. I have learned that if you are physically part of a difficult situation, rather than looking on from the outside, your "coping force" comes into action, and you are able to deal with emotionally difficult circumstances so much better. I knew that once I had seen my dad, I would be fine and would be able to cope with the problems of day-to-day life by purely being there in an active and useful way. It was just that first meeting with him on that particular day that I was overanalysing and was anxious about. Was I going to hug him? What would I say? Would we cry? All sorts of uncertainties were crossing my mind. I felt so nervous about that first meeting. How do you approach your father for the first time after just finding out that he has terminal cancer?

My brother took me to my mother's house before going on to the hospital. It gave me a chance to catch up with her. Although it was an emotional homecoming, she was visibly relieved and happy that I was there. I would be supporting her, and now she wouldn't have to be in the house on her own during those long and uncertain nights. Despite the sad situation, it felt wonderful to be there, knowing I could finally feel involved and hands-on. It was the right place to be, and strangely enough, it felt better than ever to be home in Holland.

It didn't take long, however, before anxiety about meeting my dad overpowered my feelings again. I told my mum that I was ready to make the twenty-minute car journey to the hospital, where my dad was awaiting my arrival. My mother and brother took me there in the car. I didn't speak much on our journey over there because I was again visualising our meeting in my head. I was feeling more and more nervous as we got closer. I just wanted it over and done with. The hospital was situated on the edge of our local town of Tilburg, where we parked under the canopy of some trees on the edge of a big horticultural field. It felt very Dutch. I was happy to be in my fatherland.

When I entered the hospital, it looked more like a shopping centre. The building was beautiful, with big plants, shops, and coffee shops mixed in with the usual buzzing atmosphere that you see in all hospitals. I was aware, though, that it wasn't a happy shopping trip. We were on our way to the oncology department, the one that everybody wants to walk past—the department where you certainly don't want to have to visit a loved one.

We got into the lift and stopped on the second floor. This was as far as my brother and mother would take me. They told me which room he was in so I could spend time with him alone. Walking down that corridor towards his room, on my own, I seemed to walk forever. I felt nervous and would have happily turned back to the safety of my healthy relatives, but that wasn't an option. I knew he was waiting for me, and he was probably excited to see me. Did he have similar feelings of anxiety about seeing me, or did he just want to hug his little girl while he still had time to do so? I tried to put myself in his shoes, and I could only imagine the latter. If I didn't have long to live, I would want to love and hug my children with even more intensity than I had before. I would want to sit next to their beds and watch them while they slept. I would want to put them in my pockets and carry them around, but most of all I would want to make sure they would be prepared and able to cope with their lives without me. I would tell them that our love goes far beyond the physical world.

My oldest son, Luke, was about eight years old, he asked me, "Mummy, when I die after you do, how will I be able to find you?" I told him that our love is so strong that we would always be able to find each other, that our souls are always connected from anywhere in the universe.

I stopped just before I got to the door leading into Dad's room to compose myself. In that split second, I decided I wanted to try and be strong for him, just like he would want to be strong for me. I took a big breath and walked in. I saw him, walked faster to get to his bed quickly, and hugged him while we both cried. I can still feel our cheeks touching and our arms embracing. I felt overcome by so much love for my dying father. We stayed in that embrace for at least a minute, and when we finally let go of each other and had our first real eye contact, I told him how sorry I was for the bad news. He agreed that things weren't too good. He was very emotional and kept bursting into tears. He was clearly having to come to terms with the bad news. I sat down and took his hand, and we just looked at each other and cried for a minute or so longer. After a few minutes, we composed ourselves and were able to talk about what had happened to him. We talked about the technicalities of the operation, his wound, and the future. He told me he was determined to fight this cancer and have the maximum amount of "gifted time" allowed.

Suddenly life seemed so worthwhile, and the intensity of this meeting that had given me so much anxiety beforehand was powerful and life changing. Nothing about it was superficial, and from that moment on, I knew that my father was transforming the bad news of the terminal cancer by asking, "How can we make the most of this gifted time?" We didn't know how the journey would evolve, but I knew then that whatever would happen, he would always try to have his glass half full. I was praying that the pain would be under control for the remaining time he had left because a glass can't be half full if you have to deal with severe pain and the suffering it brings.

Weblog: Friday, September 29–Toon, Jr.

We have just come back from visiting Dad and feel things aren't going too badly. He can feel that his intestines are slowly coming back into action and felt great when he was able to let off some farts. He is not totally bedbound and was spending some time in a chair.

We talked about football and the stock market, and he told me where he wants his bed to be when he gets home: Downstairs, in the lounge in front of the window, with lots of light and with a view of the village green with its beautiful oak trees. He is positive about the time he has left, and it's an absolute pleasure to visit him. By being optimistic, he manages to also make life a lot easier for his children and grandchildren. He has emotional bouts, but overall, his smile and positive outlook win the day.

Weblog: Saturday, September 30–Dianne

I have been with Dad in the last three days and have found him emotional after the news that his cancer is terminal. But he is also at peace with the situation. Of course the emotions are important to be able to process the devastating news of his cancer being terminal. Today he seems to be feeling much better, and his pain relief has been reduced to just paracetamol. He was able to sleep on his side for the first time in months. He has some withdrawal symptoms from coming off the morphine; they should subside soon, and hopefully this is an indication that the cancer in his large intestine is not in the way and causing pain anymore. That would be some good news. I have to go back to England now and am planning my return trip in three weeks' time. I have a feeling that he will feel much better by then and that we will have some real quality time to look forward to.

SUNDAY, OCTOBER 1
SIXTEEN DAYS AFTER THE DIAGNOSIS

Back in England, I allowed myself to get on with my day-to-day life as my father was recovering from his operation. I felt that in the short term, things could only get better. Knowing I was going back to see him in three weeks gave me peace of mind and time to come to terms with the reality that I had to prepare myself to let him go. I grounded myself and managed to cope by doing crafts for the school Christmas fair and by taking myself on many reflective walks. My dear friends and especially my children and husband gave me much-needed love, comfort, and support during this emotional time. I often found myself silently grieving out of the blue; tears would just come rolling down at the most unexpected times.

Weblog: October 2–Toon, Jr.

Have been to visit Dad two days in a row. He had a really difficult day yesterday and felt very sick, he couldn't keep any food or drink down, and he was restless. Apparently it is quite common to have a setback on the fourth or fifth day after this kind of operation. Last night was reasonable again, and he slept well but only with the help of stronger painkillers. This afternoon, I visited with my mum, and he seems much better again.

Weblog: October 4–Toos

I left the hospital happy for the first time today. Although Toon is still tired, he is positive, and the pain medication has been reduced again. We also enjoyed a little walk around the ward together. There will be another meeting with the doctors tomorrow. When Toon comes home, we are planning to make the time that he has left nice and peaceful. We have reached an age of self-discovery, when we can appreciate the small things in life. Thank you from both of us for all your healing words and best wishes.

Weblog: October 5–Dianne

I call my dad every morning. Today he sounded positive and told me that he is feeling stronger every day. The pain is not totally under control, but the doctors are working hard to get this balanced. He is hoping to come home at the beginning of next week.

Weblog: October 5–Peter

A meeting with the surgeon took place this afternoon. The recovery from the operation is going according to plan. The oncology team has discussed Dad's case, and the advice is to start chemotherapy to control his symptoms. A meeting about the pros and cons of chemo will take place with an oncologist on 17th October. Until then, we should focus on the recovery process from the operation.

It is decided that the pain will be controlled with morphine plasters as of today. If the pain settles down, Dad is expected to come home at the beginning of next week.

Weblog: October 7–Christian

Visited Dad this evening with my wife and our two children. Things are looking up, and he is looking forward to coming home, where he wants to inhale the fresh country air. He is also quietly hoping to take up his daily swims. These are the types of wishes we like. He wants to come home and pick up where he left off at the beginning of July. All three of his sons live within 300 meters of his house, so by the end of next week, he should be able to walk to all three addresses for a visit. I am looking forward to welcoming him.

This evening, he played cards with his grandchildren. When we left, he asked us to turn the TV on so he could watch football. Dad has gotten his taste for life back, and he has to wait only two more nights until he can come home.

Weblog: October 8–Peter

We expect many of you will want to visit when Toon when he comes home tomorrow. Of course we will be delighted to see you all, but please, please don't all come at once. Toon needs a lot of rest and won't be able to cope with streams of visitors.

We would like to instigate short visits in the morning from 10:30 a.m. until 11:30 p.m. If you want to visit, please call beforehand and also on the morning of your visit to double-check that Toon is up to it. We find that every day is different and unpredictable.

Toon and Toos send their love to you all.

Weblog: October 9–Dianne

Dad came home today and has loved being in his garden while the sun was shining. He prefers being home now and has enjoyed eating my mum's dinner. No place like home…

Weblog: October 11–Christian and Peter

Dad has been home for two days now. The first night was very difficult, and pain kept him awake yet again. The doctor has addressed the pain medication again and has upped the dose. Dad is currently pain-free, but due to the loss of almost an entire night, he is very tired today. The strong medications are also making him feel confused at times.

This evening, he was determined to watch the Dutch national football match. He fell asleep five minutes into the game.

Tomorrow there will be a meeting about possible treatment with the oncologist. All in all, things are difficult. Perhaps we will have some more news tomorrow.

Weblog: October 12–Peter

Last night, yet again, Toon woke up with severe pain. Lizet (his daughter-in-law, who is also a nurse) came in the night and administered an extra morphine tablet.

This morning, we went to the hospital for a meeting. The advice of the oncologist was to admit Toon back to hospital to regulate the pain control. If any treatment is to go ahead, Dad needs to be stronger, and the pain needs to be under control. Yet again, Dad and the family had to deal with another huge disappointment.

I felt so sad for my parents and dreaded to think how they had coped during those two nights, which were yet again filled with more pain and despair. He had been looking forward to coming home so much, and now the awful pain had taken all the joy out of what should have been a really happy time. The fact that my father was suffering in Holland took its toll on me in England. My mood was very dependent on how he felt.

Weblog: October 14–Peter

Things have improved rapidly again since Dad has been in hospital. The nights are peaceful, he is enjoying the food, and he goes out on regular "walks" in his wheelchair. It's miraculous how things can change from day-to-day.

Please do contact our mother, Toos, if you want to visit.

Weblog: October 15–Toon, Jr.

Just came back from the hospital where we took dad on a lovely walk through the local park surrounding the hospital grounds. You could read the enjoyment in his face and he was able to name all the different types of trees in the park. He was feeling on top of the world today and cherished being outdoors.
A scan of his abdomen is scheduled for tomorrow, so that they can trace the area that is giving him so much pain.

Weblog: October 17–Christian

Toon is doing well in the hospital. He shares the ward with three other people, and they enjoy chat and laughter, and behind closed doors, probably also tears together. In the afternoon, we took him for a walk in his wheelchair, which has become the highlight of his day.

Today's scan was very painful, but thankfully that pain is now under control again. On Thursday, Ans, Lizet, and Mum and Dad have a meeting with the doctors to discuss the result of the scan that was made today.

Weblog: October 19–Ans

A meeting took place with Dr. van Riel, the oncologist, and the ward doctor, during which the state of play was discussed. The scan didn't give them any more information on top of what they already know.

It's been decided that he will go home over the weekend to give it another try. He will go back to the hospital on Monday, when they will hopefully strengthen him and control his pain enough so he can go home later next week for definite.

We were also told that treatment won't be possible while Dad is so weak. At this stage, it's all about quality of life and palliative care. A friend left a message on his weblog today that says, "The most important thing is to keep the fire burning through love, kindness, and care," which is what we as a family are going for.

Weblog: October 20–Christian

My mum and I have just returned from the hospital, where we had a lovely time with Dad, chatting about all sorts of normal daily subjects. It was really refreshing. Peter is picking Dad up tomorrow morning, and hopefully he will enjoy the weekend at home. Things appear to be well controlled with regard to pain medication. He has been making plans for what he would like to be doing while at home, so fingers crossed all will be well for him. Wishing all readers of the blog a very good weekend, too! We are feeling positive.

Weblog: October 22–Peter

We collected Dad from the hospital yesterday morning, and he is enjoying being at home at the moment. Yesterday we made a visit to Christian's house, which was followed by a peaceful night. The pain seems to be managed at the moment, but what we need now is for him to have a good appetite.

This morning, his brothers, Theo and Janus, came for a relatively jolly visit, which was followed by a nap and a trip in the wheelchair through the village with some welcoming chat with some village friends. He is currently watching football and is feeling excited because Dianne and her family are arriving from England in about an hour's time. Soon after she has arrived, we will take him back to the hospital.

OCTOBER 22
FIVE WEEKS AFTER THE DIAGNOSIS

Dad was waiting for us at home and was thrilled to see us, but I was shocked to find him looking like a gravely ill old man. The children sat themselves on the sofa, quietly observing the new-looking Opa in an innocent state of disbelief. In their eyes, their fun-loving, active Opa seemed to have expired. He sounded the same, but his voice was weak. He smiled the same, but due to his weight loss, his false teeth didn't fit him anymore, which resulted in him having no teeth in his mouth. That made him look like a different person. He had pain written all over his face. It was quite shocking for us all to take in this transformation, but we soon realised that he was still in there somewhere and managed to crack a few jokes with the boys, which lightened the mood a little.

I was astonished that somebody could deteriorate like he had in just three weeks. Last time I saw him, he still looked relatively healthy, but not now. After about twenty minutes of being together, my brother came to take him back to hospital. My mother and brother lovingly wrapped him up in a warm coat, hat, and scarf and helped him up from the edge of the bed. Once he was up, they had to hold him tightly while he slowly shuffled to the front door. He barely had the strength to keep upright. It was painful to watch, and I had to turn my head away to hide my tears. My strong father, the head of the family, looked so weak and vulnerable, and it really hurt. I realised that night that his life was drawing to a close much faster than we had anticipated.

OCTOBER 23
A DAY OF CONTRAST

My brother, Toon, and I travelled to the hospital that morning to accompany my father to a bone scan, which would determine whether the cancer had spread to his bones. We took him to the X-ray department and had to wait our turn, just like everybody else. I looked around at the other patients and couldn't help wondering what their stories were. There were about twenty people. I guessed that eight were patients and the rest were loved ones accompanying them in the waiting room. Not much was said, and most were quietly engrossed in their own thoughts, most possibly suffering with their own emotions. The room was filled with anxious energy. It was a welcome little break when my dad needed to go to the toilet. It meant a distraction from the nervous wait. He couldn't manage the toilet on his own anymore, and I was happy to take him. He used to joke with us and say, "I'm glad I have five children so when I'm a little old man, unable to look after myself, at least one of them will probably help me clean my bottom." That helpless old man had appeared far too quickly. But I would honor his wishes. It made the task a bit easier that day because in my mind I had already been there. My father wasn't at all body-conscious, never had been, and he was used to his painfully thin body by now. His other children had already been helping him with going to the toilet. I just had to follow my siblings and not make a big deal about it. It was sad and challenging, though, to see and feel his bones through his skin. It was a reality check of how painfully thin he had become. I could tell how grateful he was to have me there, and although it was a difficult task, I was also grateful that I was there to help him. Once I wheeled him back to the waiting room where my brother was still waiting, we didn't have to wait much longer until his name was called.

Having the scan was painful for him, and it was hard for my brother and me to watch. He had to be moved around into angles that his sick and painful body couldn't easily achieve. It was a relief for all three of us when it was over. It felt like a real treat to be able to go for a walk outside afterward and get some much-needed fresh air.

We were yet again blessed with a beautiful, crisp autumn day. After an initial little stroll around the hospital grounds, we walked on a bit further to a nearby canal, where we sat ourselves on a bench along the edge of the water. We quietly sat there watching the boats, barges, and cyclists go past. It felt peaceful and special to sit there with my father and brother. There was no need to speak, and just being there on the edge of the canal was meditative and thought provoking at the same time. We enjoyed this state of real contentment and appreciation of each other for half an hour or so before we set off again. We walked past a little old chapel and decided to go in to light a candle. There was no need to say who we lit it for. Ever since we were tiny children, we have visited chapels and churches to light candles and pray for sick people. It's an important ritual I still do to this day with my own children. It makes them stop and reflect, just like my dad, my brother, and I did as we silently sat in this peaceful little place of faith. It was an immense contrast from what we had just come from, when we were sitting on the edge of the canal, watching normal, day-to-day things in life pass us by. This chapel, or perhaps you could call it God's house, felt more like the halfway house to the hereafter. I'm not sure which was more special for my father: the day-to-day life he had to let go of so soon or the spiritual life in this chapel, which felt peaceful and safe somehow. He was looking quietly down on the chapel floor made out of mosaic with a pattern of little black and white tiles, perhaps symbolising the mixture of the light and the darkness.

OCTOBER 25

I was glad that my visit wasn't a short one this time and that we had six whole days in Holland. My brother, Christian, let us use his holiday home just a five-minute walk from my parents' house. This enabled me to spend time alone with my parents while Pete, my husband, and the boys did other fun things. Although my father was happy to be in his home environment, he did still have to suffer a lot of pain. At this stage, he was self-managing the pain medication and found that if he took too much morphine, he would, in his eyes, sleep excessively. He wanted to make the most of being with his loved ones during the time he had left. He would be fine for a couple of hours, and then the pain would kick in suddenly and intensely. During the pain-free hours, there was real time of enjoyment when we went for walks in the wheelchair. He would have happy chats with the locals and could enjoy some sense of normality. However, a lot of the villagers had also started to read the weblog which was accessible to anybody. Therefore, we also felt very much watched by the locals. We would sometimes see them peeping through their windows as we walked past. We were understandably the main story of the moment in "the village chatter." They were feeling sorry for us and were wondering how much time he had left. It meant that everybody could choose to be hooked on our story of life with terminal cancer.

The flip side of this was that people genuinely wanted to make a little bit of a difference for my family. The messages and acts of support from within the village community were overwhelming. We also received many communications from friends around the world who would be checking into the blog and sending us messages of support from afar.

Early evening was often the time when the pain would intensify and when I would give my dad a Reiki treatment. I used to do voluntary work in my local hospital on the oncology ward, giving the patients healing, so I was used to giving people with cancer Reiki healing. It was difficult to do it for my own dad when he was in so much pain. There wasn't a single position he was comfortable in, and this made it hard for us both to relax. But we persevered because it did improve his general well-being. Healing doesn't mean being cured of an illness; it is about finding inner peace, calm, and acceptance by balancing your energy within.

I experienced mixed feelings of relief and guilt in the evening when I left my parents' house for the night in exchange for a comfortable holiday home with my healthy husband and children. It was so important to have this time away to cope with the situation and find some inner peace for myself, something I found hard to do while my father was so uncomfortable with the pain. I just wanted him not to have to deal with the pain so that he could have peace in the remainder of his life. I remember reading a line in a poem once that said, "Pain brings you closer to God." The way his illness was evolving, I felt that that day would come sooner rather than later.

Weblog: October 26–Toon, Jr.

I'm afraid to say that recovery is not the order of the day. The quality of the nights is deteriorating, and he is yet again trying to sleep in an upright position, to no avail. This morning, we walked three miles through a local woodland estate called "de Utrecht" with him in his wheelchair. He thoroughly enjoyed it. The afternoons seem to be his best part of the day. The moments of real enjoyment, though, are getting scarcer.

OCTOBER 27
SIX WEEKS AFTER THE DIAGNOSIS

My week in Holland was going too fast; only two days remained to spend time with my dear father. When he wasn't in pain, he was totally at peace and accepting of his illness and short-term fate. Good friends and family came for short visits to say their good-byes, and it was obvious how shocked they were to see him so thin and frail. One friend who hadn't seen him for about twenty years walked into the lounge and asked, "Where is Toon?" while he was sitting right there in front of him. I can't even begin to imagine how this must have felt for him. During these visits, he would talk bravely about his illness, shake their hands, and thank them for all they had done and had meant to him in his life. Most people would then put their arms around him and start crying, often bringing their own baggage to my ill father, making it even harder than it already was. Every time I witnessed this, I wondered if we would have a proper good-bye or if he would die when I was back in England. Only time could tell.

OCTOBER 28
A LANDSLIDE WIN

It was a beautiful day, and the sun was shining upon us accompanied with the Autumn smell of the ripe earth. My husband Pete, our two boys, and I took Dad out in his wheelchair to watch two of his eight-year-old grandsons play in a Village League football match. The two footballing nephews probably knew the chances were high that it was the last time their grandad would be there to watch them play football, the sport he had such a great passion for. I'm pretty certain that they wanted to play the most amazing match just for him and do him proud. They sure didn't fail in their determination and managed to win the game 13–1. We all enjoyed watching my dad having a wonderful time and feeling so proud. It was as if the clock had turned back just for a little while, and life was as it used to be. Right then, the sense of joy was so much more intense than it ever had been. When there was light, it would be so very beautiful and bright. The contrasts in this journey with cancer were immense, and the fact that life is a dance between joy and pain was more evident than ever.

OCTOBER 29
KEEPING IT SIMPLE

It was the day of our departure, and I was relieved that I had already planned to come back to see Dad in ten days' time, just so I was able to say "I will see you next week" when our time to say goodbye came. Anything could happen between leaving and coming back, but I had a gut feeling that it wouldn't be the last time I saw him. That thought certainly made saying goodbye easier that day.

He was sitting in the garden, waiting for me to come and say goodbye. I didn't want to overanalyze the moment, so I just walked up to him, kissed him on the cheek, said, "See you soon, Dad," and left. Somehow for me that was the best way of coping with our goodbye. It was protecting both of us from more unnecessary emotions. We both knew the possibilities. I felt that my father was letting me guide the parting that day, and I chose the lighter option. The thought that overshadowed the journey back to England was anxiety about how he would look on my next visit. For now, though, I was pleased that I was travelling back to my safe little haven in England, physically away from all the troubles that my family were enduring in Holland. It felt like a guilty escape, but honestly, I would have much rather had them living nearer to me so I could go and see them anytime I liked. Living such a long way away felt harder than ever.

Weblog: October 31–Peter

For a change, the doctor had some good news and told us that the cancer hasn't spread to his bones. She says we should still aim to strengthen Dad's health.

Dad wants to thank you all from the heart for your support and healing messages. So many of our friends look at the blog on a daily basis and share their feelings with us. Some of you lovely people continue sending us messages. It means so much.

Extracts of some special messages received during this time

"What you share as a family is unique and something to be proud of. Togetherness gives strength, something needed during these difficult times. From Cathy."

"It's been a nice, sunny day here at Mistletoe Cottage with blue skies and the smell of freshly cut grass. From Peter."

"Toon, we got to know each other in the hospital, and I was inspired by your positive outlook on things, which gave me strength. Thank you for that. Dineke."

"I read your blog every day but don't always know what to write. But perhaps the thought that people are sharing your journey with you gives you strength. Enjoy your time at home inside and outside the house. Bas."

"So grateful for Internet so I can feel close to what is happening from America. Your god-daughter, Carin."

"Autumn is a second spring when every leaf is a flower (Albert Camus). Lia."

"I hope your memories in life give you joy. A friend like you is a gift, and you have a place in my heart that is available to very few. Thank you. Ger."

"You celebrate love, and that is a gift to us all, Lou Lou."

"Never give up on your dreams, even if somebody tells you that you don't have a hope in hell, Toos."

Weblog: November 3 –Ans

Autumn, the time of the year when the colors are breathtakingly beautiful, is when most leaves fall off the trees. Some of them will persistently hold on until the cold winter kicks in, but eventually they will all have to let go.

Humankind doesn't know beforehand when their time will come to let go of the tree of life. Dad is in a stage of his life now where he is very aware that his leaf is slowly letting go. He can't rely on his body anymore; it is clearly failing him.

We don't know when the time of letting go will be, but we trust that this moment will unfold itself like a flower that opens itself toward the light.

This means that he is lingering in a place of transition, between the world of the earthly home and the world of the hereafter. He has to let go and detach himself of everything he loves. Of course it is the same the other way around for our mother, his children, grandchildren, and other family and friends who care for him.

Besides the tiredness, pain, and other ailments that this illness brings with it, there are also many things he still intensely enjoys. The daily walks with his dearest family in beautiful countryside, with which he has always felt very connected. Watching robins and blue tits that enjoy the treats left out for them just outside his window. Little touches, hands, playing cards, cosy homemaking by my mother, warmth and love from all the people around him.

35

Weblog: November 6 – Christian

This past weekend was difficult, and I am pleased to report that today seems a little better. The days but especially the nights were plagued by extreme pain for Dad and was torturous for both our parents. The doctor has readdressed the pain medication and has yet again had to increase the dose. Slowly but surely, we are all becoming more and more aware that the end is nearing fast. I hope we will still be able to enjoy the small and simple things in life together and that the pain can be kept under control.

NOVEMBER 7
SEVEN WEEKS AFTER THE DIAGNOSIS

It was becoming harder to live my daily life in England. My dad was clearly deteriorating fast, and I was wanted in Holland. I felt restless and detached from the situation and felt that I needed to be there. It was also easier to cope when I was there with them. The situation at home in England was difficult because my heart was very much in Holland. I didn't feel I could share my love with my boys the way I should, and I felt irritable and sad. My father was too sick to speak on the telephone, and all the information I got was secondhand. I wanted to be with him, hold his hand, sit with him, care for him, and cry with him. Being together with my parents certainly made the process of accepting the coming of death easier. I decided to bring my trip forward.

Weblog: Wednesday, November 8–Christian

Our father taught us to always be preventive, which is also the case with pain medication: "Don't wait until you hurt, but act earlier." It's a little trick he has recently learned. After all, you should practice what you preach! His last three nights have been comfortable for him whilst in his own bed, something he hadn't been able to do for months, so that in itself was quite an achievement. There isn't a chair in the house that he hasn't tried to get comfortable in, often to no avail.

This week, he enjoyed a glass of his favorite cognac. Dianne is coming home from England tomorrow—something to look forward to. We pick the day and make every single one count.

Thank you to all our friends and family for your continued support; it makes a difference.

NOVEMBER 10
SEVEN AND A HALF WEEKS AFTER THE
DIAGNOSIS – GIFTED TIME

When I arrived back in Holland, my fears about his physical deterioration were confirmed. His mental strength, however, was impressive and had grown. Because the pain appeared to be under control, he was able to transfer all the energy that he had been using for coping with pain into something so very beautiful called love. Love for the small things around life in general but also love for his family, who were so very precious to him and from whom he would soon have to part. He told me that he didn't find it hard to let go of life but that letting go of us, his children, wife, and grandchildren was the most difficult.

During the day, friends and family were popping in and out to say their good-byes. Most people were aware, mainly due to the blog, that the end was nearing. As a result, good-byes were definite. He had come to the stage where his body was actively dying of the cancer. Saying farewell and letting go of these people was emotionally exhausting for my father, and it put a huge daily strain on him. We didn't want to turn family and friends away; we wanted to give them the opportunity to come and say goodbye. Perhaps it was more for themselves than it was for my father. It is part of the process of life, and although it was emotionally difficult, we felt that we didn't have to make this journey on our own. The care and love, but also the distraction, made those weeks when he was visibly dying more bearable.

During the calmer parts of the day, he was quiet and told me he needed peace. I had so much respect for the way he was so calmly and serenely dealing with the final phase of his life. He was teaching me a lesson, for which I will be forever grateful. The lesson was not to be scared of death but to embrace all that is in life. Don't try and distract yourself out of a difficult situation, but really experience the feelings that come with being close to death. I'm convinced that my father's final journey will give me strength when I reach the final phase of my life, and I want to follow his example as a gift to my children.

NOVEMBER 11
EIGHT WEEKS AFTER THE DIAGNOSIS – LAST RITES

It was the day that my father chose to have his last rites with all his family by his side, while he could still be consciously aware of this important Catholic ritual. The last rites are the last prayers and ministrations given shortly before death. Pete came over with the boys from England because he genuinely wanted to be there. We were all grateful that he made the long journey to make the family complete.

We wanted to make these last rites spiritual and beautiful for him, so we decorated the lounge with flowers and candles. We were ready for the ceremony, which was to be held at eight o'clock that evening.

I was nervous because I had never been present at such a ritual, and I wasn't quite sure what to expect. I had often heard my parents talk about friends and family getting their last rites, and ever since I was a young child, I had a vision of what that would be like. In my mind, it was a grueling experience that took place in a dark room with a bed in the middle. In it would be a very sick person, and around the bed would be a serious priest with wailing relatives not wanting to let go. No wonder I was nervous to enter my parent's house just before 8:00 pm after the short walk from my brother's house.

When we entered the house, my father was lying in his bed in the middle of the living room. All of the children, in-laws, and grandchildren were gathering and sat in a circle around him. It was certainly an occasion, with all twenty-two close family members present. It could have been Christmas, or Easter time, when we would usually all be together, but this time, although it felt warm and loving to all be together, it wasn't a celebration. My father had his hands in prayer position, and his presence was strong. He was like a spiritual rock carrying us even then, on his deathbed, through the ritual of the last rites. My father's ego had been dropped along the way during his illness, and all that was left lying in that bed was a body of purity that was in transition between two worlds while being surrounded by love and light. He looked like a tiny, old, wise man who was totally at peace with what his future had to offer him. It felt like there was only one transparent layer between the two worlds of life and death.

The last-rites ritual wasn't at all what I had always dreaded. The room was filled with positive energy and, although we were sad, we were also joyous to share this momentous occasion with everybody who really mattered in our lives. My dad had consciously volunteered to be part of this ceremony. It was an occasion of mixed feelings. The presence of the grandchildren made the occasion light and less serious. The priest gave them little tasks and let them light the candles and help him carry the cross. We were all aware why we were there, but we chose to be in the moment and not think about the near future too much. I was wondering what went through my father's head during all this, knowing that it would almost definitely be the last time he would have all his loved ones by his side. His mental strength was admirable. In his lifetime, my father had learned to sail in many winds. I am not sure whether it was for him a night of storm or calm, or perhaps a wind he hadn't had to deal with before, but he certainly knew how to sail it.

After the ceremony, I was content about how special and beautiful the evening had been. In a funny sort of way, it felt like one more thing ticked off the list of things to do before somebody close to you is dying. There was a sense of acceptance and knowledge that the day would come soon, and when it would arrive, we would all be at peace about it. I believe that this journey of my father's illness was a life-changing experience for all of us.

NOVEMBER 12
MEMORIES

It was Pete's birthday. He would be traveling back to England with the boys. Therefore, it would almost certainly be the last time he would see my dad alive. He, too, went to visit him for "final goodbyes" before they set off on their journey home.

My dad asked to spend some time alone with Pete. He was sitting in his wheelchair and took Pete's hands in his hands, knowing damn well that it was the last time they would ever be together. The main message to him was not to chase his dreams but to be happy and content with what he had. Pete is one of these people who wants to climb the next mountain once he reaches the first. I understood and appreciated my father's message to him.

It was hard for me also to say goodbye to Pete and the boys. I decided to stay for a couple more days because I realised that time spent with my father was becoming more and more precious.

After Pete and the boys left, I spent the rest of that Sunday afternoon with my parents and my sister, watching old home movies from happy times when we were young children. They were fragments of our life as a family that only we share. It felt like we were able to step back thirty years in time, when we didn't appear to have a care in the world. Our family holidays, when all seven of us got packed into the car like sardines in a tin. Picnics right next to the fast roads, with only the occasional car driving past. Getting the cows in at dusk for milking. Our dog, Bruno, my two younger brothers, and me happily bouncing behind the cows through our fields as they slowly made their way to the "night-night shed" where my father would milk them while we made swings and huts out of hay bales. My best memory of all was when the roads had frozen over and we were able to skate from village to village. The dogs didn't understand why they weren't able to stand up. Watching those home movies, I sat next to my dad on the sofa and sneaked glimpses at the expressions on his face. I wondered what was going through his mind while he watched his life go by on the screen. Did he feel his life had been worth living, and did he have any regrets? Was he longing for those days when he was young, strong, and healthy? It was emotional to watch, and mixed feelings crossed all our minds, I'm sure. But I felt warm and grateful to have my dad there close to me on the sofa on that memorable Sunday afternoon, knowing that these were some of the last precious times we would share together.

We realised and concluded that Dad couldn't be left on his own during the night anymore. He needed support to go to the toilet, and somebody needed to be there just in case anything serious happened. My brothers, sister, mum and I were taking turns. That night, it was my turn to sleep in the living room with him. My mattress was on the floor only a few meters from his hi-tec hospital bed. I didn't like the idea of spending the night with that responsibility next to somebody who was so very ill. I was extremely anxious about what could happen. It did make him feel at peace with me being there, though, and I told him I would be there, just meters from his bed, should anything happen. We said our goodnights, but it took me a long time to fall asleep. I kept checking his breathing to make sure he was still alive. I must have eventually fallen asleep and was woken up at about 3:00 a.m. by his call for help. He was in a lot of pain and needed to have a dose of morphine, which I administered by mouth. I sat on the bed with him for twenty minutes or so, holding his hand and rubbing his back while waiting for the pain to subside. We didn't talk, and experiencing this discomfort in the middle of night with him made me realise how difficult those first undiagnosed months must have been. Once the pain had settled down a little bit, I took him to the toilet, which was also heartbreaking. I was holding him in my arms while he slowly shuffled toward the toilet. His trousers were so loose that I had to hold them up around his back or they would fall down his legs. It was upsetting to see him suffering like this. We finally made it to the toilet, and I rubbed his back while he was sitting down, still in a state of extreme pain. I felt the bones sticking out of his skin. Being there at that time in the morning with my dying father was tough. No light, distraction, no escape from the reality. This was the now, and this was difficult. On the one hand, I was grateful that I could be there for him in his darkest hours, but on the other hand, I would have walked away from the situation if I had a chance to. I think if I had been a nurse and this sick person had been a stranger or friend, I could have dealt with it much better, but the fact that this was my father with the role reversal that was taking place made this whole night so much more emotionally demanding. I eventually took him back to his bed, where we sat together for another twenty minutes or so until his pain subsided. I was glad to crawl back into my temporary bed and eventually fell asleep again. I was relieved to hear him breathe, knowing he had survived another night, when I saw the light peeping through the curtains that next morning.

For four months, he had been having painful and disrupted nights, and this was the first one I had witnessed. The experience made me realise that in comparison, the days were so much easier. The nights must be a lonely and dark place for terminally sick people. It is when the mind wonders off to the unknown.

NOVEMBER 13
PRESCIOUS MOMENTS

It was my last full day in Holland before I had to leave again. Cooking a breakfast for my dad and myself of toast and a boiled egg, the one meal he still got a little enjoyment from, was so easy in comparison to the previous night that I had endured with him.

I remember that morning well. He had no pain. Our favourite piece of music, the Stabat Mater by Pergolesi, was playing while we sat on the sofa together, both eating our egg and toast. Nothing was said; we just felt intense love for each other. We were both aware that these were some of our last precious moments together, and being there with him that day was intense and special. I felt closer to him than ever and knew that our time together was coming to an end. These were some of our last glances at each other. Soon these warm hands I was holding would be cold, and my father's body would be an empty shell. Soon he would be entering a new world. I was hoping that his new world would be filled with love and peace just like we felt that morning.

NOVEMBER 14
BEING TOGETHER FOR THE LAST TIME

My very dear friend, Ria, was to pick me up at 10:45 a.m. and take me to the train that would take me back to Brussels and then on to England. After the nurse washed and dressed my father that morning, we wrapped him up warmly and sat him in the wheelchair. We placed it next to an empty chair for me to sit in, in a warm and sunny spot in the garden. It was ten o'clock, which meant I had only forty-five minutes left to spend with my father before my departure. I asked my mother if she would mind going for a walk so I could have some time alone with him which she willingly did. I said goodbye to her and sat in the empty chair next to my father. I took my father's hand in my hand. We quietly sat and enjoyed the beautiful garden that he had nurtured and loved for so many years. There was the warm and familiar smell of autumn leaves that made a blanket around us on the ground. The birds appeared to be singing exclusively for us, and it was peaceful to sit there while holding his warm familiar hand. I didn't want to be anywhere else. I felt overcome by love while being there with him on that beautiful crisp autumn morning.

I said, "Dad, is there anything that still needs to be said?"

He answered, "No, my darling, I have always loved you so much. There's nothing more to be said."

I'm certain that we both knew that it was our last time together. I said, "Dad! I can be here in four hours. If anything should happen to you, I can travel fast if I need to."

He replied, "No, you belong with your children in England. If anything happens, you don't need to be here."

His saying that brought me such relief. I was so grateful to him for not putting any pressure on me. We sat there in silence for a bit longer, and it felt like time was standing still. We were both so grateful for each other's company, and all was well.

My mother returned from her walk far too soon and told us it was almost time to go. My friend, Ria, arrived, and suddenly I needed to think about getting my things together. I suddenly got ripped out of a beautiful state of being with my father, and so was he. My father, with his sharp mind still intact, was explaining to Ria how to get to the train station more quickly. Amazing, in the course of just a few minutes the whole atmosphere changed.

A few minutes later, it was time to say goodbye. I needed to be strong for my father, and I knew that he was going to be strong for me. I gave him a long and big tight hug. The warmth of his body transmitted love and sadness at the same time. Although we didn't mention it, we both knew it would be our very last embrace. Nobody knows what's waiting around the corner in life, but on that day, we knew. It made our goodbye extraordinary because it felt like we were consciously opening the doors to our inner souls. I realised before his passing how very dear and loved he was, and experiencing that so intensely with him was extremely precious. After our embrace, I walked away from him. I wanted to have one last look at him. I stopped and turned around. He blew me a kiss. I blew him one back.

As soon as I got in the car on my way to the station, I burst out crying. I was glad Ria drove me to the station so I could share my feelings with her. She is my oldest and one of my very dearest friends.

Having her there made the transition between saying goodbye to my father and travelling back to England on my own easier. I told Ria that the goodbye to my father felt like the last one ever.

Before I boarded the train, Ria gave me a special bag filled with goodies for the journey. She told me not to open it until the train had left. Having caring friends like Ria really helped me on this journey of letting go of my father. I kissed her goodbye and boarded the train.

When the train pulled away, I looked in the bag and found a massive bag of heart-shaped sweets with a loving note from my special friend. Her caring gift put a smile on my face.

NOVEMBER 15
TWO MONTHS AFTER THE DIAGNOSIS

As always, it felt good to be home with my boys, and I was relieved that my father had taken the pressure off me by telling me that there was no rush to get back to him in a hurry if he took a turn for the worse. He said I belonged with my own little family in England. That made me feel it was OK to live my life and do what kept me focused on normality. I certainly felt that I needed some downtime with my children and husband after a very intense week in which I had felt the love for my father more intensely than ever. I also needed to be with my children to help me get through this difficult phase in my life. They were giving me so much unconditional love, normality, routine, and distraction, which was just the type of therapy I needed. They made me realise how lucky I was to have them. It made me see what I had in the way of secure and unconditional love and a future after my father's inevitable passing, and with it, my loss of his unconditional love for me. I needed to be home with them to recharge myself for the next phase, which I believed was just around the corner.

That afternoon, I went to a friend's house and had lunch and very welcome laughter with girlfriends. It balanced my energies somewhat. There had been so many tears in the previous week that I needed to lighten it. I know my dad was trapped with his illness, but I was still young, and there was no reason for me to deny myself some fun in my life, too. I was lucky to have four siblings who were now taking their turns looking after him.

I felt good at the end of the day, although my thoughts were still very much with him a lot of the time. I shed tears just like I did on most days, but I felt that I had been given guilt-free permission to live as normally as I possibly could.

I rang home late that afternoon, and my mother told me that Dad had had a good day. His best friend had visited, and he even drank a glass of beer, accompanied by laughter and a friendly chat. My day felt fulfilled, my dad and I both enjoyed fun and laughter that day, and I went into the evening feeling warm, calm, cosy and relieved to be home.

It was around nine o'clock in the evening when my brother rang and told me that Dad was experiencing severe abdominal pains. The doctor was called. He decided to give him a morphine injection. The pain didn't subside after the first injection, so the doctor decided to give him a second. His heart rate was high. I told my brother that I wouldn't rush back; I played my dad's words in my head from the previous morning, when he had told me not to rush back if anything were to happen. I was in no state to drive all the way back to Holland that evening. I thought that if he were to die that evening, I would forever treasure the last time I saw him when he blew me that memorable kiss.

Nobody knew what the night would bring, but I had a gut feeling that this night could be the time of my father's death. I wanted to and had the opportunity to be there with him in spirit through universal energy and sent him long-distance Reiki healing for about two hours. I could feel the energy flow and knew that this Reiki energy had a calming effect on him. It also made me feel very much connected with him.

I went to bed around eleven o'clock, relieved that I hadn't had any more phone calls. I hoped that my dad would make it through yet another night. The two hours of Reiki had also balanced me, and I managed to settle into sleep quickly.

The sound of the phone woke me up at 3:30 a.m. in the morning. My heart was already beating in my throat. I tuned into reality instantly, and I knew what this call was about. I had mentally prepared myself for the possibility of this call in the middle of the night for quite a few months. My husband was awoken instantly, too, and switched on the light. The phone was on his side of the bed, but there was no question as to who should answer the phone; we were both struck by instant anxiety. I picked it up and heard the voice of my sister saying, "Are you OK?" I knew the next line and wanted her to just say it. "Dad died about an hour ago. I wanted you to know as soon as possible. You might be able to connect with him, as his energy is still very near."

Even though I was prepared for the call, it was upsetting and shocking when it came. The realisation that I would never see him again felt real and unreal at the same time. I told her, "Thank you for letting me know. What should I do next? Shall I get up now and come to Holland?" She said there was no hurry and that I should just stay in bed for now. I said goodbye to her, and we agreed to ring each other later that day. My first instinct was that they shouldn't have rung in the middle of the night. It all felt really surreal, especially because I wasn't there to be part of it all. If I had lived just up the road, it would have been easy to just walk or drive over and be with the rest of the family. But being hundreds of miles away across the sea made it all complicated. I followed my sister's advice and stayed in bed, initially. It was hard to comprehend the news. I could still so easily hear his voice and visualise his smile. I was wondering where he had gone as I imagined his soul travelling up away from us. This was touching me on a deep level.

I cuddled up in Pete's arms, crying. It was good to have him home. He was a comforting support that night. He also loved my dad dearly, and it was a great loss to him, too. About half an hour later, when the initial shock was wearing off a little and when my body was able to relax and be at peace with the fact that I was in my bed rather than in Holland, I started to "feel" as my sister suggested. I had an amazing experience of real peace and saw yellow and blue circles pulsing in my inner eyes. I felt calm and serene, and it was an amazing experience that lasted for about three minutes. To this day, I believe it was a sign from my dad telling me that he was with me in spirit. This experience gave me a real sense of peace and acceptance about his passing. I had been preparing for his death for more than two months and felt relieved that he was finally without pain.

While I continued lying in bed, I was mulling over my sister's words. Dad had fallen into a deep sleep around nine o'clock the previous night while I was giving him Reiki. That was a nice thought. My mother, two of my brothers, and my sister-in-law, Lizet, had been with him during this time. They had been reading to my father from *The Book of Life and Death* by Rinpocha and poetry by Hans Stolp about letting go of life. Although my father was unconscious for hours prior to his death, he had waited for my sister to get home. When she finally arrived, she told my father it was OK to let go. She also told him that everything is love. He died very calmly and beautifully only thirty seconds after she arrived. I was pleased for her that she had made it just in time. She told me that after my father's death, she helped wash and dress him, a ritual to aid in bereavement. This would have been something I would have had great emotional trouble with, so in a way, I was very much at peace that I was in my own bed.

I couldn't get back to sleep, and the phone rang again at five o'clock that morning. It was my brother, Christian, who was on a business trip in England. He had only just heard about my father's death and was still in a state of shock. He hadn't been able to say goodbye to him properly and wasn't sure how to get back to Holland fast. He said he wanted to go with me, but he was in Cambridge, a three-hour drive from our house in Kent. I booked him on a flight from Stansted Airport near Cambridge to Eindhoven that left at seven o'clock that morning, glad he was on his way so he could be with his loved ones at home. Now it was time for me to decide how I was going to make my way back to Holland.

3

Dad's Final Goodbye

Weblog: November 16–Peter

Our father died at quarter to three this morning, with his loving family
by his side.

His death was still rather sudden. He had a great day yesterday.
Drank a beer and shared some jokes with a good friend.

Around 5:30 p.m., he experienced severe abdominal pains that were
difficult to control. The doctor gave him a large dose of morphine.
From nine o'clock onward, the pain subsided, and he managed to
fall asleep. From 2:00 a.m. onward, his health started to go downhill
quickly. He died peacefully with his family by his side. He has
managed to let go of life and was at peace with this. His family is also
at peace with their loss.

It was a controversial blog message, but I agreed with my brother,
Peter, and felt very much at peace with my father's death. He didn't
die alone, which was a blessing in itself. I took great comfort from my
experience a few hours earlier, when I saw the beautiful colours through
my inner eye that I believed my father gifted to me. My interpretation
of that vision was that all was well.

The night moved into dawn, and dawn moved into day, and with that transition came practical reality. There was the daunting thought of unpacking the suitcases that were still filled with dirty clothes from my return only days earlier, followed by more packing, with the added work of packing smart clothes for the funeral. Travel tickets would also have to be booked. But first of all, I would have to break the news to my children. They were due to wake up soon.

It was such a contrast yet again from going into the evening so calmly the night before to another extreme of packing and travelling, without having even a moment to come to terms with my father's death. I was functioning on autopilot.

The children took the news in their stride, and both wanted to give me lots of cuddles, which was lovely and comforting. I was more grateful than ever to have two beautiful boys by my side. I felt blessed to have children of my own. I was determined to take them to school that morning, and from there I would continue my journey to the train station and on to Brussels and beyond.

On our two-mile car journey to school, my eldest son, Luke, asked me, "Mummy, where is Opa now?" I stopped the car in a place of exceptional beauty with an exquisite view. We looked over the familiar, beautiful, and tranquil Kent countryside of rolling green hills, which we are blessed to see on our way to school on a daily basis. I asked the boys to look at the beauty around them. I pointed out the old oak trees that Opa was so fond of and reminded them how Opa used to say that if they could speak, they would have some interesting stories of wisdom to tell. We looked at the rolling green fields, dotted with fluffy sheep unaware of this day being any different than all the others. The skyline made the contrast between heaven and earth, blending together in ever-changing moods of light. I told the boys to take in and appreciate all this beauty that we sometimes take for granted. I told them that Opa is everywhere that's beautiful. We all were quiet for a few minutes while each of us dwelled on our own thoughts. That very field we looked at that day is to this day called "Opa's Field." The most beautiful footpath runs through it, and I know we all still think about him and feel him in spirit as we cross this scenic field on our walks to school.

No more questions were asked that morning, and I was pleased that my answer satisfied their hunger for knowledge about death.

I dropped the boys off at school and kissed and hugged them goodbye, knowing that they would come and join me in Holland a couple of days later. I was getting used to leaving them behind, something my father thought was a good thing that had come out of his illness.

I shared my loss with some supportive girlfriends at school before I set off on my journey to Holland. Somehow I felt in quite good spirits. I know this sounds contradictory, but I was marking an occasion, the death of my father. It was a day I had been preparing for, and I had obviously done a pretty good job. I didn't have to deal with great shock like many others do when a loved one dies suddenly. I felt blessed by the fact that I had an amazingly powerful final goodbye with my father only two days earlier and was relieved that I wouldn't have to see him in pain again.

My kindhearted neighbour brought me a gorgeous bunch of flowers, and friends called me to offer support and help. I enjoyed all the attention I was receiving and felt that I was being carried by caring friends, particularly on that day when he died. My husband took me to the train station and waved me off.

Soon after the train pulled out of the station, I started sending friends texts about my sad news. I wanted and perhaps also needed this attention. It was touching to receive all their comforting replies. A few hours into the journey, as the train was getting nearer to Holland, I was feeling more and more uncomfortable about arriving home. One of my oldest and dearest friends, Emma, who had been the girl next door during most of my childhood, sent me a text from Cape Town, South Africa, where she still lives. Emma and my dad had always had a lot of respect for each other, and she thought so much of him. Her text read, "The village will never be the same again now he has gone." This message really hit home, and with it, the realisation that Dad had really died genuinely kicked in. From there onward, my train journey was filled with tears. I felt quite self-conscious but couldn't control the outpouring of my emotions. Other passengers must have wondered what was the matter with the crying lady in their carriage.

When my train eventually made it to the familiar Turnhout station, I was relieved to see my younger brother, Toon, waiting at the station for me yet again. We embraced each other. This time it was different. We had reached a new phase. We were now dealing with death as opposed to dealing with a very sick father. Yet again, though, just like only a week earlier, he seemed remarkably together and was dealing with the death event in a remarkable way. Yet again it showed me that being amidst the reality of difficult times is easier than watching from the outside.

On the half-hour journey to my parent's house, Toon told me about an amazing experience he had when Dad died and how it had really changed his spiritual belief. My brother's hand had been on top of my father's head when he took his last breath. Immediately after the moment of Dad's death, Toon felt heat being released from the top of my father's head, which my brother strongly believed was his soul making an exit. I was happy for him but also for me because it was another possible sign of the hereafter. Perhaps we all get signs in different ways. They certainly made coming to terms with the loss a lot easier.

As my journey home drew to an end, I was growing more nervous and anxious. My friend, Emma, was right: coming home would never be the same again. When the car pulled into the drive and my brother turned off the engine, I found it hard to open the car door and make the final part of my journey. I knew damn well that the hardest part was the final part of my journey—walking through the door of the house where my father was laid to rest and the difficulty I would have to face once I entered. My brother said, "Come on, Dianne! It has to be done." He gave me a little mental push, which was just what I needed. He led the way to the door and opened it, giving me no other option than to walk in.

Unexpected visitors were in the house—people from the village who came to offer their condolences. I didn't want to be confronted with those visitors and went no further than the hallway. I burst into tears. The realisation that my dad would never welcome me home again hurt. I could hear his voice saying, "Hello, my girl. So glad to see you."

My sister and my mum came to my rescue and embraced me. I felt pain from the depth of my heart while I was releasing my tears. I embraced my mother tightly and buried my face in her shoulder. Despite being in the safest place I could possibly be at that time, I was still very aware that to the right of me was the door leading into the room in which my dead father was laid to rest in a coffin. After a minute or so, my sister asked if I was ready to go and see him. I was panicking and told her that I was too scared to face seeing my father dead. My experiences of viewing dead relatives as a child had caused me trauma, and I couldn't even begin to comprehend what it would be like seeing my own father dead. She tried to convince me that it wouldn't be traumatic at all and that she had had an amazingly positive experience by the coffin earlier that day. Even her lovely experience didn't change my fears. She told me that I may regret it if I didn't go and see him and that it's best to do it straight away. I eventually but reluctantly gave in. After all, it really is the thing to do in my country.

My sister held my hand as she slowly opened the door that would lead us to my dead father. The first thing I focussed on was the sea of flowers on a table behind the coffin that had a candle burning in the middle of them. A strong aroma of flowers mingled with an unfamiliar smell, which I was later told is the scent of embalming. After focusing on the flowers and candle, I was aware that there was no more distraction from the coffin that was standing right in the middle of the room. My eyes had to readjust to look at my father lying in it. I was shocked when I saw him. He looked like a white rubber doll lying in frilly white satin material. All I was thinking of was how quickly I could run out of that room. My sister, who was still holding my hand, suggested that I confront with my fear of dead bodies by calmly looking at him. This did help a little. He was holding a white rose in his hands and was wearing his cosy red woollen cardigan.

My eyes were fixed on his hands that were holding the rose. Those hands that I had been holding only two days earlier when they were warm and comforting had now transformed into cold, motionless, waxy-looking hands. Those hands had been such an important dimension in my life. They had worked hard and had brought the food to the table, they had punished me during naughty times in childhood, they had played the guitar during happy family times and they had comforted me when he was slowly dying only days earlier. Those very hands were still there, but their intent had ceased. The spirit of my father had gone. His eyes were closed, his lips rigid and cold. His face was like a mask, but still I could hear his voice. I was wondering where his soul had gone. I couldn't sense what my sister experienced by that coffin, and I just wanted to get out quickly. But out of respect for my father, I stayed longer than I wished for.

I was glad when my sister decided we had spent enough time with his body. I was overcome with mixed emotions when I slowly walked out. Looking back now, I am glad I saw him in that coffin because I would have probably spent the rest of my life wondering if I had done the right thing had I chosen not to go in. Seeing his body cold and dead made me realise that he would be alive in my heart always and completely. People say it's part of mourning and letting go. It can help you move on. I'm not sure if that's true, but I'm pretty sure that if I hadn't seen his body, I would have always wondered about it. I rarely think of my father in the coffin when I think of him. I remember him how he was—before the cancer, mainly.

My mother was being strong for me and had a welcoming coffee ready for me. She made sure that the friends who were there when I arrived had gone home. It meant that we could have some privacy. We talked about my father's passing and all our different experiences since his death. I could feel a sense of relief from all of my close family members. After twenty minutes or so, I was told we had to prepare for the wake on Sunday and the funeral on Monday. It is customary practice in Holland to have a funeral over and done with within three or four days after death. My sister and I were given the job of writing a reflection about our father, on behalf of his children, that would be printed on the back of his photograph and handed out to people attending the funeral. The two of us went upstairs for some peace and quiet. We sat around a little table and looked onto the land where we grew up. We sat quietly for a while, gathering our thoughts. Once we got the ideas into our heads and got into the flow of writing it down, we composed the following ode to our father:

You were a colourful, exceptional, and striking human being and were strongly connected to nature and stood, rooted like an oak in all its beauty taking its place in an open field. You would always show yourself in your true colours.

You walked your own unique path and wouldn't be influenced by others. You enjoyed taking others on your path, sharing your ideas and inspirations.

You were a man with many talents and possibilities and worked hard for your family, your business, organisations, committees, and village life. In the past twenty-five years, you chaired "De Brinkdansers," the folk-dance group, and inspired the other folk to dance through life with a smile on your face. In this, you shared your life slogan: "Always think positive."

You took any opportunity to travel around the world and enjoyed learning about different cultures, which broadened your outlook on life and people. Your wife, Toos, allowed you to travel to your heart's desire and would always support you in this.

Apart from your earthy common sense, you would follow your intuition. You relied on this in all your life decisions, and this led you to a search about the meaning of life. In the last ten years of your life, you were reading many books about spirituality and in your own unique way had many conversations with God.

As a father, you taught us many important lessons, for which we are grateful. Many of your sayings and beliefs are engraved in our hearts and memories and will no doubt be passed on to our children. For your children, you were fundamental and were seen as a rock among burning chaos. Because of this, we felt balanced as human beings who were able to fly in and out of our nests at all times. You would always encourage us to spread our wings without fear but to never forget to land.

As a grandfather, you would open your heart. Your grandchildren enriched your life and brought you much happiness. Every single one of them adored you. With them you swam, cuddled, rumble-tumbled, played cards, and went for many walks. Never a negative word about any of them.

In the last phase of your life, your heart became softer. All layers were removed, and your feelings streamed. It was a worthwhile process for all the family. Life had taken you to the heart of life in which you found beauty and amasement in all life around you.

We remember you with gratitude.

We were pleased with our liturgy, and the rest of the family approved. Everybody got little tasks to get on with, and it felt good that the funeral and wake were starting to take shape. Spending time with all three brothers, my sister, and Mum in this way was pretty precious. It was a warm feeling for all of us to be able to share the same grief for the man who had been carrying and shaping this family the way only a father could have. That day proved just what a good job he had done. We were all pulling together to give him the best possible send-off and felt strong as a family.

As the evening approached, we felt a real sense of achievement knowing we had planned a considerable amount of the funeral. We spent the evening reminiscing about our beloved father. There was a lot of unexpected laughter, and wine was flowing infinitely. During those initial days and weeks, we were all grateful and happy, even, that my father was relieved of his pain and that we had been released of the "on hold" and unknown period of time that terminal cancer brings with it. Soon we would be able to get on with our lives again. It would be a life without a father, and that would be uncertain in itself, but we would at least be able to have normality and routine, which had been so very scarce in the previous three months.

When my siblings left to go to their own homes late that evening, it was just my mother, me, and my father's body left in the house. I didn't want to leave my mother on her own and offered to sleep in her bed with her. She said no and felt she would be OK. I personally didn't like the idea of sleeping in the house with my father's dead body, but I managed to pull myself together and rise above my fear. At least I was sleeping upstairs. The coffin was downstairs, on the opposite side of the house. It took me hours to get to sleep. It had been a long and intense day, with many contrasting emotions and impressions. At about 3:00 a.m., I was woken up by loud Gregorian chanting, which genuinely scared the hell out of me. I had no idea where this sound was coming from. My heart was beating fast, and I was too scared to get out of bed to see where it originated. It was eerie, and I thought perhaps it was a sign from my dad again, which I thought was not convenient or well planned at all. After fifteen seconds or so, I realised that the sound was coming out of my mother's CD player in her meditation room next to my bedroom. I ran over there quickly and pulled the plug out and then shot back into my bed, my heart pounding. To this day, I don't know why that happened. It was such a scary experience, and the only rational explanation is that my sister had pulled out the plug of the CD player when we were writing that afternoon in that very same room, messing up the timer, and it went off in the middle of the scary, dark night.

NOVEMBER 17
PLANNING THE FUNERAL

The light that morning had never been more welcoming after that unwelcome and terrifying experience during the night. It was the first morning in a long time that I was able to go down the stairs without the added anxiety of wondering how Dad would be. It was all too often during my visits in the previous couple of months that I would find him downstairs in much pain. Instead, there was the hustle and bustle of funeral directors, siblings, and well-wishers. Such a contrast with three mornings ago, when quiet classical music was playing in the background while my gravely ill dad and I were eating boiled eggs on the sofa and feeling the intense love and emotions that went with that morning I spent with him.

It wasn't like that the day after he died. It flew by as friends and family came by for well-meant condolences and hugs, which were accompanied by tears but also laughter as we remembered my father. Further work was done toward the preparations for the funeral and the wake. In the evening, myself, my brothers, my sister, and my mum spent more lovely and warm time together, reminiscing. It felt so important to share this time together, and I was amazed how lighthearted this day had felt. We were all united with just one focus: my dad's funeral. We all wanted it to be amazing, the best send-off ever that he so truly deserved.

NOVEMBER 18

How pleased I was to wake up that morning knowing that Pete and the boys would be joining me. I was starting to miss them, especially the children, because they were such a comfort to have around at that time. They were young, eight and four, but their feelings were pure, and I was amazed at their intuitive behaviour with regard to my feelings.

They would stay at my brother's holiday home while I would continue to stay with my mum at my parents' house.

I felt complete when they arrived that afternoon. We asked the children if they wanted to see their granddad in the coffin. The younger one, Henry, said yes, and the older one, Luke, said no. I respected both of their choices. It made me realise that even at their young ages, grieving is so individual, and there is no right or wrong way. I was grateful that my husband took our son in to say goodbye.

I wrote a little poem about the last few moments that my father and I shared, which I would read at the wake:

A last glance, I will never forget.
You blew me a kiss, and I blew you one back.
An invisible kiss that was deeply felt.
Daddy, you are now also invisible, but I feel you deep, deep in
my heart.

That evening, after the wake, friends and family were invited to pay my father's body their last respects. We placed candles leading up to the house for people to be guided to him. It was a quiet and moving affair. Some people would come and go, and others would come into the living room and share their condolences. It was a healing and spiritual experience. Friends and family would share their memories, just like we had been doing within our close family during those days leading up to the funeral.

After nine o'clock, when all the guests had left, we decided to put the lid on my father's coffin. We all felt that we had said our goodbyes and were ready for closure on that front. The body was also deteriorating quite rapidly. It was a spur-of-the moment decision that we siblings and my mother should put the lid of the coffin on together, in a kind of symbolic way. I was hesitant to go back into the room where my father was resting but felt obliged to do so and didn't feel that I was in a position to refuse.

The grandchildren and in-laws went in first to say their final goodbyes and put their drawings and special gifts in my father's coffin.

Then it was just us, his children, and our mother left. We went in together and surrounded the coffin. We all just stood there looking at him, and again I felt uncomfortable. One brother suggested we should all help put on the lid and screw one of the screws in to secure it on top of the coffin. There were seven screws, which was the number of people in our family, with five children and a mum and a dad. But my dad couldn't participate. Suddenly it felt like I had landed in a Monty Python comedy. My brothers were making pretty sick jokes like, "Come on, Dad, get that screw in!" It was a surreal experience, the last time we had the opportunity to see him, a major moment, and my brothers made light of it. It was a coping strategy, I suppose, that probably worked for them.

Of course the jokes were funny, and it's good that tears and laughter go hand in hand. We all composed ourselves and got serious when the screws were attached, although secretly I think each of us thought that the whole experience was slightly strange and quite hilarious. All sorts of emotions were provoked during those days, and humor was one of them. It took the sting out of death.

NOVEMBER 19

The days were starting to drag on. I wanted closure and was wishing it was Monday, the day of the funeral. I was ready to put my father to rest.

My mother was coping remarkably well. Like my father, she had suffered so much over the past months. She had nursed him and had been with him at all times. The only bit of release she had had was the odd walk or quick shopping trip out, so initially after my father's death, there must have been some kind of relief for her, too. A lot of the mourning had already been done because we knew his cancer was terminal. When you know you are slowly losing somebody, you prepare for when they will be gone. I have spoken to other people who have lost loved ones to terminal illness, and they all say the same thing: that initially after death there is a sense of relief.

The wake that evening was very moving. I chose to play a piece of music on the piano by Eric Satie. With the emotions running high, I was nervous when my time to play the piano came. When I sat down on the piano stool and put my hands toward the keys, my fingers were shaking. I felt unable to play. I closed my eyes and called on my father to help me. I felt a sudden calm come over me, and I managed to play the piece beautifully. Family and friends came up to me after the service to tell me that I played in a beautiful and serene way. One even said that I had played like an angel. I believe that I had to thank my father for this, and I felt empowered by the fact that my calling had actually been answered. The service was moving. His children and grandchildren read poems and played music. It was a welcome hour of reflection and tears that took us into the final phase of saying goodbye before the imminent funeral that was to follow the next day.

I went off to bed early knowing that the following day would be big.

NOVEMBER 20
DAY OF THE FUNERAL

Today it was my turn to walk behind the coffin, being viewed by onlookers while walking up the church aisle. I wanted to look my best, not only out of respect for my father but also because many friends and family I hadn't seen for many years would be attending the funeral.

The hours before the funeral took place were busy, with funeral directors coming in and out, getting everything ready for the service at twelve o'clock. The family members were arriving, and we were getting ready for the church. It was all a great distraction from what was about to come, when the moment of real intensity and seriousness would arrive. We were all doing our thing, getting flowers ready to go to the church and making sure our clothes all looked decent and smart. There was even a slight sense of excitement in the air. For me this came to a sudden halt when I glimpsed through the window and saw the big black hearse parked on the green. It was parked outside our house. It wasn't moving; it was waiting. It knew it was at the right address. It was here to accompany us on our dark day. The day you wish on nobody but everybody has to experience at some time in their life. The day you fear when you see the funeral parade going through any town or village. Today was definitely our day, the day we had to say goodbye to our dear father. This was genuine and serious, and at that moment I broke down in tears.

I was soon stopped in my tracks. It was time to guide my father's coffin out of the room he had been lying in and into the waiting hearse. This was a serious and momentous happening. My brothers did the honours and couldn't help making a little joke when the trolley on which the coffin was placed couldn't quite make the turning out of a narrow bit in the hallway. They said, "Dad really doesn't want to leave the house." In the end, the coffin came off its trolley, and the funeral directors and my brothers carried the coffin out of the house with full respect and gently slid it into the hearse. All the family gathered around the hearse and waited for the funeral directors to put the flowers on and around the coffin. It was quiet, and all eyes were focused on one thing only. I imagine that we were all thinking similar thoughts, about this being the last time our father would ever leave the house. The sad thought that he would never come back haunted me. We would never again enter our parental house and see him. All these issues certainly crossed my mind while waiting for the hearse to leave.

This was a challenging moment of realisation for all the family. The church bells were ringing their somber funeral melody in the background. The atmosphere had become quite serious. The hearse drove off slowly, with the family following it for the five-minute walk to the village church. While walking behind the hearse, with the church bells ringing in the background, the whole village stopped what they were doing and stood still, paying my father his last respects as he was making his final journey to the church. I was having my own thoughts about the times I walked this road to the church when I was a child, holding my father's big, warm hands that gave me a great sense of security. I remembered the times we walked down this road only weeks earlier when my father was ill. He had kept strong to the very end, chatting and waving to those very villagers who had now stopped what they were doing to pay their last respects. Many cars were parked along the road, and this was a sign that the church would be filled with people. This was a comforting feeling.

We got to the church a few minutes before midday and were greeted by the folk-dance group in full uniform. He had spoken to them weeks earlier about his wish for them to escort him into the church at his funeral.

They lined up in couples and entered the church, followed by the coffin carried by my brothers followed by my sister and myself being either side of my mother, followed by the rest of the family. When we entered the church it was consolatory to see it so full. My father's wish was to have a sung requiem. My brother-in-law who is a conductor and his musician colleagues sang the Gregorgian chant of requiem Aeternam by Mozart beautifully. The music was powerful but angelic at the same time. The angelic presence in the music made it feel so right. I knew that the service would feel like the perfect transition between life and accepting death. It did also sound so very sombre and whilst walking up the church aisle my eyes were focused on the coffin at all times. All I could think of was that this was the last time my father would be with us in body. I felt extremely strong and carried by love all around me. It was a very powerful experience.

When we got to the front of the church I sat down in the front row with my mother in between me and my sister. I was the very nearest to the coffin and my eyes were fixed on it.

The Gregorian chant was mesmerising, and it enabled me to think about the memorable times I had shared with my father. It gave me the opportunity to dream of special times gone by. I was starting to have to compose myself five minutes or so into the service to prepare for the first reading, which I had written myself.

I walked up to the microphone in the nave of the church calmly and had an emotional moment for a few seconds before I was able to start reading:

Dad, with thanks and gratitude, we give your body back to the earth. We are grateful for who you were. To us, you were like your favorite tree, the oak, which you will be associated with from this moment on.

The great oak amazed you over and over again with its symbolic expression of years of life experience. You used to say, "What a beautiful tree. I wonder what this tree has witnessed in its life."

The oak stands in the earth, deeply rooted and sapping the earth's nutrients to be able to grow strong in a way that you also stood strong and fed yourself from nature. You were also fed by people you met along the way. The combination of nature and people helped you grow spiritually. Just like the acorns of the oak tree can grow into a new oak wood, you also took care of your wife, children, and grandchildren, whom you loved more than anything.

Dad, we are so grateful for the things you taught us. You always saw the positive in people. You taught us not to be scared of things but to face them. You made us appreciate the small and precious things in life.

In the last phase of your life, you taught us another great life lesson. Together with you, we made contact with death. You made us experience that death is not something to be scared of, but instead, you made it a peaceful ending of a beautiful life on earth. Your approach in the final stage of your life was a gift, and I would like to thank you for this.

My reading was followed by my sister singing "Vergiss mein nicht" by J. S. Bach.

The funeral service was beautiful and sincere. I didn't shed many tears and felt empowered by my extraordinary strength while feeling a strong connection to my father as I was sitting near his coffin, even though I was very conscious of the fact that it was our final goodbye. Losing a parent is the one thing you fear as a child, and I was astonished by how well I was coping on that particular day. He still felt very much a part of my life because the love I have for my father hadn't died and is still here today, strong as ever, seven years to the day of his funeral while I write this book.

Walking out behind the coffin to the music of "Paradisum" by Gabriel Faure through this long church aisle and in view of everybody was overwhelming. My sister and I walked with our mother. I felt extremely vulnerable while people looked at us in an unintended intrusive way. Although I knew that everybody meant well by showing their empathy and support, at that particular moment, I would rather they hadn't been there and would have preferred walking out of the church in private. I felt very much on display.

I was relieved to have made it to the church exit, only to find that the heavens had opened, and rain was pouring down heavily. It was my father's wish for the folk-dance group to play some happy tunes as the procession made their way to the churchyard, which was a welcoming contrast to the rain and the sadness that was so strongly felt by all attending. Once all were gathered around the coffin in the churchyard, a good friend of my father made a warm tribute. The priest said some words, after which friends and family all walked around the coffin, paying their last respects. We, his immediate family, stood by watching them all in the pouring rain. I was grateful that Pete and the boys were there offering me much-needed support. This was certainly one of the saddest days in my life.

When it was just his nearest and dearest left in the churchyard, each of the grandchildren were given a balloon, and they all let the balloons go up into the sky to join Opa in heaven. It was a beautiful and light moment, and it was a comforting thought that in the eyes of the grandchildren, those balloons would join my dad in heaven.

The downpour had made the soil on the graveyard wet and slippery. When my brothers and Pete helped the funeral directors lower the coffin, Pete slipped and got a foot in the grave. Luckily somebody managed to pull him straight out. Emotions were running high, and we couldn't help but all have a bit of laughter about it—a great coping mechanism and release at that particular time. With the giggle left behind us, we went into serious mode again and circled the grave, said our goodbyes, and left flowers on his coffin. We all felt content that my father had had a great send-off and that we would now be able to grieve his death and move on with our lives. We felt united as a family, and with the rain pouring onto us, it was OK to leave the churchyard and our father's body behind us and join our family and friends in the village pub, where my dad wanted all guests to have lunch and drinks on him. It was a good gathering with a mixture of tears, laughter, and memories and a great opportunity to reconnect with long-lost friends and family.

Initially after his death, we were all grateful for normality and routine in our lives again. My mother threw herself into creativity as an antidote to possible depression. As the months went on, visits from friends and family became scarcer. Most people presume you should be OK by then. The time came for my mother and for all of us left behind to experience the emotions within. We were no longer able to hide behind the distraction and had to come eye-to-eye with all the emotions that were stirring within us. I was finding solace in the daily life of my children, feeding and nurturing them more so than ever, and my mother had her sculpting, meditating, and Reiki. The hardest thing for her was coming home alone at the end of the day.

After my father died, I started phoning my mother every day, always at times when I knew she would be alone. Even though we talked mainly about sweet little nothings, we both valued these calls, and it helped both of us through our grief.

Our bereavement was made bittersweet because we had been able to say goodbye to my father, and most of the experience was spiritual, filled with hope and faith in the everlasting. We lived toward his death as a family united in love and care for each other. If his death had been instant, it would have felt like a sudden storm that caused chaos and destruction. In our case, it was a slow-moving shadow where the cloud caused some darkness and sadness but after accepting the inevitable, a silver lining of light appeared.

I have my precious and meaningful memories of those months during his terminal illness. I was able to give my father's death closure with gratitude for the "gifted time" we were blessed to have had. I had my intense moments of grief, but I never felt that he had totally gone. All that was left of him were memories and love, and that got me through the months following his death almost effortlessly. I felt his light shine on me from wherever he may be. His qualities and his being and all those things lost were manifesting themselves within me. His absence made itself known in me. It was the inheritance amid the grief. He worked within me by making me strong and loving.

4

Sudden Deaths and New Life

NOVEMBER 17, 2008–VENTURES NEW, TWO YEARS LATER

It was two years to the day since my father's death in November 2006. About a year after his death, I decided to do something positive in his memory. I wrote a children's book called *Remembering* that's intended to help children with their grief when they lose someone special in their lives. I was fortunate to find a publisher (Child Bereavement UK) soon after I finished writing it. It has turned out to be a beautiful little keepsake book. In it are the most beautiful drawings, illustrated by my friend, Daniel Postgate. To this day, it is still serving its purpose, and many children have benefited from working through their bereavement in a creative and personal way with the help of my book.

It was nominated and highly commended by the British Medical Association and was reviewed and praised in the national press by Richard Madeley and Judy Finnigan.

We were a week away from signing the book contract with Child Bereavement UK. There were many stressful last-minute changes going back and forth. I was dependent on other people to make those changes, and it caused a lot of stress for me in different ways. I had a disagreement with one of my good friends with regard to the book one day, which made me feel sad and powerless. I was already vulnerable because it was the second anniversary of my father's death.

I stood by the sink in my kitchen and looked out of the window, when my eyes wondered off to the little picture of my father that was standing on the window ledge. His face smiled at me, inviting me to pick it up. I looked at his face and realised that he felt further away than ever. I started crying. I felt empty and lonely, and I missed him more than ever. I talked to the picture and asked him to help me. When he was alive, he would always have some good practical advice to give, but instead of his good advice, I ended up sitting on the kitchen floor, holding his photo between my legs, head down, tears rolling down, with a feeling of extreme loneliness. I sat there for about ten minutes like that before I was forced to pick myself up to get ready for the school run.

When my husband came home from work that evening, I was really pleased to see him. We have our issues as a couple, just like all other married couples with children, but at the end of the day, he is still my best friend with whom I can share everything. The evening ended beautifully with intimate lovemaking, and all was well.

NOVEMBER 30, 2008
BOOK-CONTRACT SIGNING

I woke up early in an unfamiliar environment at my brother-in-law's house. It was a cold and frosty morning, and I was cosy in bed, wondering with excitement about the book-contract signing later that morning. Some time passed before Pete's only brother, Dave, brought me a welcoming cup of tea. Pete is one of four siblings. In his family, there were also their twin sisters, Margaret and Elisabeth, who had recently celebrated their fiftieth birthday.

Dave kindly let me stay at his house, only a few miles from Child Bereavement UK's headquarters, where the signing for *Remembering* was to take place. It was only a children's book, but it had been a long time in the making, so it was a big day of achievement for me. I felt really proud of myself because my determination in getting the book finished and published had paid off! That day, I finally could let go of my book project and let the charity take over in the hope that the book would serve its purpose of helping children through bereavement.

I said goodbye to Dave and made the short journey to West Wycombe, a quintessential little village just outside London. In true "me style," I arrived about an hour early and browsed the welcoming little gift shops in this cute village, trying to distract myself from nerves. Christmas was coming soon, and I have a compulsive tradition that I have to buy a new Christmas decoration annually to remember that particular year. I bought two reindeer candleholders that would remind me of that particular year. I thought signing my contract was a memorable day, and buying those little reindeer in that particular village was appropriate. I didn't realise then, on this happy day filled with excitement, that another momentous moment was still to come in 2008.

DECEMBER 7, 2008
DAD'S ENERGY

I said goodbye to some good Dutch friends who had stayed with us for a couple of days, during which lots of drink and food was consumed. I treated my friend to a Reiki session, during which she sensed the presence of my father. She told me that she felt like an intruder picking up these vibes because, in her opinion, this energy exchange was something between my father and me. I was intrigued but didn't think anything of it at the time.

DECEMBER 9, 2008
AMAZING NEWS

I am pregnant! On the sad day of the anniversary of my father's death a few weeks earlier, when I had held my dead father's picture and asked him for help, I had fallen pregnant. My friend felt my father's spirit only a few days earlier, and I could only conclude that this pregnancy was a gift from him. We had talked about having another child because I had this niggling feeling, but Pete was not keen. He felt we were too old for another child, but he was happy to just give it one go. He said that if it was meant to be, it would happen. This one chance was given in the evening on the anniversary of my father's death. It certainly was meant to be. A little spirit had chosen us in the only opportunity it was given in seven years, when we had used no contraception.

I really hadn't expected to fall pregnant and found it hard to get used to the idea of having another child. My husband was the one who was happy, but I just couldn't feel it and was in shock and denial. The following day, when I was on the phone with my mother, she asked what was wrong with me. She had been thinking of me, and she knew me well enough to know something was up. I burst out into tears and told her, "I'm pregnant, and I'm not happy. I won't have enough hands to hold three children, and my two boys will be missing out, as a new baby will take up all the time…" My mother interrupted my outpouring, telling me that the best gift I could ever give my children was another sibling. My mother's words gave me peace of mind and certainly helped me cope better in the days, weeks, and months of severe sickness to come.

The due date of our baby was on the same date as my nephew, my brother's son, Chrisje, who had been born stillborn eleven years earlier. Could all this really be coincidence, or were they all signs?

It didn't take long for the morning sickness to kick in, and I spent the weeks leading up to Christmas on the sofa, looking like a corpse that would only move to be sick in the toilet. The pregnancy was tough. I was feeling extremely sick and tired, and it was difficult to feel grateful for having been gifted another child.

We decided to tell the boys about the pregnancy on Christmas Day. It felt appropriate because baby Jesus was very much on the scene. The news of their very own baby at Christmas would, as my mother said, be a real gift to them.

A week before Christmas, the boys were starting to ask questions. They were concerned about me being so sick and wanted to know what was wrong with their mummy. I told them that I had had this illness before. They didn't buy it and wanted to know what this illness was called. I couldn't delay the news any longer and had to tell them. Their reaction was amazing. They gave me the biggest smiles ever, and my mum turned out to be right—what better gift was there for a child than another sibling?

AUGUST 17, 2009
BABY FINALLY ARRIVES

Rufus arrived nearly two weeks late, after twenty-eight hours of intense labour, ending on August 17, 2009. A beautiful big bouncing baby. I felt elated. The love I felt for him when he was put into my arms was immeasurable. All was well.

Growing from a family with two children to a family with three children was quite a shock to the system, though. The work increase was extreme. I felt like an octopus being pulled in all directions. I needed my family more than ever, and although my Dutch family popped over from Holland for a few days here and there, Pete's family was also there for support.

I married into my husband's family at the age of thirty-one and inherited an additional family, including two sister-in-laws. My father-in-law was German and in the Hitler Jugend from a young age, after which he was forced to join the German army during the Second World War at the young age of seventeen. He was shot and taken as a prisoner of war to Scotland, where he met my English mother-in-law, who nursed him. She had already lost her parents and sister, and life hadn't been easy for her, either. She was extremely focused on her career as a district nurse and midwife and had continued to put her feelings aside. They had four children, my husband being the oldest, followed by his brother, Dave, and the twins, Elisabeth (Liz) and Margaret (Mag).

The two boys went to public boarding school, and the girls went to independent day school, a considerable financial sacrifice for the parents to make. Dad found solace as a psychiatric nurse, where his own war-related trauma might have gone unnoticed. Mum focussed on her career and supported the family in a material way. She was the most charitable, kind and helpful person I knew, but she was unable to confront emotions of any kind, apart from laughter. As a result, any issues arising in the family would be laughed off. The twins didn't have the easiest of upbringings, and Elisabeth suffered with mental health problems. She used to run away from home and went missing sometimes, perhaps a cry for attention. In her early twenties, she disappeared in the wintertime and wasn't found until days later. By that time, her legs had been affected by gangrene. Both her legs had to be amputated below the knee. She was diagnosed with manic depression and schizophrenia. She had a few relationships that were too stressful for her, so she stayed single and struggled for most of her life. Margaret got married in her late twenties and was blessed with three children and a loving family. She suffered with childhood diabetes, which became more of a handicap for her as she got older.

At their relatively young age of fifty, something terrible happened. The following section is short and was a very dark experience to live. I chose not to relive it in too much depth in this book.

OCTOBER 17
BAD NEWS

Rufus was two months old, and we were turning the corner. Things were starting to get slightly easier, and some sort of routine was emerging.

On this particular Saturday in October, the boys and I were driving back from a windswept and fun afternoon by the seaside, and we were all looking forward to spending our Saturday night with pizza and family entertainment on the sofa in front of the telly. My husband was working, which was pretty normal on a Saturday.

I was admiring the spectacular view from the top of the North Downs only a five-minute drive from our home. I was thinking how lucky we were to live in such a beautiful part of the world. My happy thoughts were interrupted by the phone ringing. I pulled the car in next to the road and picked it up. It was Pete's sister, Mag. "Di, something's happened. Liz, (Pete's other sister) has done something, and it's really serious this time. She has tried to kill herself." I had to stop her there and get out of the car. I told the boys to stay in the car and be quiet. I asked her to tell me again. She told me she didn't have a good feeling about this and that Liz's friend had found her in her house with her wrists cut, but that she was still alive in the ICU in a hospital near her home.

At this point, the kids were shouting out of the car, not giving me any privacy, and asking me to come in and get off the phone. I walked a bit further away from the car and tried to ignore them. That was hard when the baby started crying because it was his feeding time. I somehow managed to block the children out.

Mag told me that she didn't know much more and that she would leave soon for the two-hour journey to the hospital with her husband. She felt she needed to be there for her twin. I was in shock, and the news hadn't sunk in. I told her that I would let her brothers, Pete and Dave, know. She felt it was better not to tell her parents because they were too old to make the journey.

I got back in the car and drove off. The boys wanted to know who was on the phone and why. I told them that Auntie Liz had had an accident and was in hospital and that I didn't know much more than that.

Once home, I had to feed Rufus and get him to bed. I was thinking about Pete and his brother, who were both working on a live TV show from which they couldn't just walk away. How was I going to tell them? Luckily their work was only twenty miles from the hospital in West London, where they were based. I prepared myself and plucked up the courage to ring Pete. I managed to speak to a colleague first and told him that I had bad news for Pete. I asked if somebody could take over his job of mixing the sound for a while so he could talk to me. His colleagues were very helpful, and after a bit of reorganising on their end, I got to talk to him. "I have some bad news about Liz," I said. "She has tried to commit suicide and is in ICU in Woking Hospital. Mag is on her way there and doesn't have a good feeling about it. She has asked if you and Dave can join her."

Liz had had mental problems since she was a teenager, and any news from her about being in trouble never came as a total shock. But she had never before tried to take her own life. In fact, she had been stable over the previous five years or so. Therefore, the news of her trying to take her life came as quite a shock. I was relieved at the time that she didn't have children and that she wasn't married. Her nearest family members were Pete, Dave, Mag, and her parents.

Pete went quiet after hearing the news but was also quite matter-of-fact. He said he would go tell his brother, Dave, who was working in the same TV complex. I was glad he could be with his brother at this difficult time. They managed to find cover to finish mixing their shows and would make their way to the hospital together a couple of hours later, around 10:00 p.m. I left them to it because there was nothing I could do to help at that point.

The boys and I had our pizza and watched TV as usual, but I couldn't stop thinking about what Liz had done and felt detached and powerless from all that was happening. We lit a candle for Auntie Liz, and the evening continued as normally as it could.

The phone rang around 11:30 p.m., when I was still very awake and waiting for news from the hospital. It was Pete, and the news was shocking. Liz had really wanted to die and took double action when committing suicide. She slashed her wrists and took an overdose. Her body was poisoned by toxins, and her organs were failing. There was no hope for her, and she was slowly dying. It was a dark, sad, and disturbing thought, but I was glad that all three of them were there together to say goodbye to her. It made me sad that her parents were not there, but I believe that Liz would not have wanted them to see her that way. It wasn't merely a cry for help; if it were, she wouldn't have slashed her wrists and taken an overdose. None of us had seen this coming. How was she able to overcome the emotional stress to commit this final act. It was estimated that she had laid in her house for about twenty-four hours before she was found, so it must have been a very slow and painful death. A disturbing reality was emerging for the family. She left no suicide note so questions would never be answered. You can't help thinking why she didn't see a reason to live. Was life not precious to her? Did she feel like she was a burden? Was she suffering emotional pain? Did she want to escape negative feelings? Was there no hope for her? Everybody had their own ideas about it. Mine was that she had done some voluntary work in a psychiatric hospital about a month prior to her death. I think she couldn't cope with accepting her own mental disorder of manic depression and schizophrenia while working with people who had similar illnesses. A mirror was held to her face, revealing something she really didn't like. She never accepted her mental illnesses, and I think being on the other side of mental disease and observing her own illness from an objective point of view was emotionally too stresssful for her to handle and process. She couldn't cope with it and took her own life. I don't know if that is a fair analysis, but nobody will ever know for sure. For me, being able to come up with a potential reason why she did it helped me deal with it. But it didn't take away from the sudden devastation that it caused her family and friends.

OCTOBER 18, 2009

Early on that Sunday morning, after her brothers and twin sister had said their final goodbyes, the machines were turned off, and Liz died.

We were all in shock and couldn't really comprehend what had happened. Auntie Liz was dead. There weren't really any tears. We felt paralyzed, incapable of crying, and in total shock. Henry was upset because he realised he didn't have a godmother anymore. Rufus still woke up in the night, breastfeeding continued, and the new life of baby Rufus gave us much comfort during those difficult days, weeks and months to come. It kept us focussed on life and we were fortunate and blessed to have this new baby to love and to cherish.

The cremation a couple of weeks later was healing. We arrived early and had a little walk through the crematorium gardens before the service started. Our little family with three little boys, Pete's mum, sister Mag and her husband and children. While we wandered around the grounds a cat strolled with us and was weaving around our legs. It was a humbling thought that it might be a sign from Liz because she loved cats so much.

The service was busy and it was nice to know that she had many loving friends. She lived a couple of hours drive away from the rest of the family and we weren't really part of her life there and didn't really know much about her social life. Just like her mother she gave a lot of her time to charity work and we knew that she was a good and kind person.

Her twin sister Mag wrote and read a very moving tribute about her sister. I couldn't help thinking that she must have felt torn in half.

The weeks that followed were particularly difficult for her surviving twin Mag. She wasn't coping very well at all. Her diabetes seemed to be spinning out of control and she had more hypos than ever. On some days she would walk into our house appearing healthy, and within ten minutes of being totally normal she would be slurring her words and slowly be passing out. Large amounts of sugar would help her get her back to functioning normally again. It was a very emotional time for her. She wasn't really coping with the loss of her twin. She was wearing her sister's clothes at all times. She sought help from a bereavement counsellor but continued to struggle physically and emotionally.

DECEMBER 5
SIX WEEKS AFTER LIZ'S DEATH

We had got over the initial shock of Liz's death and were starting to be able to give it a little place in our hearts. Pete had a busy job, and having three boys and the house to run gave us plenty of distractions and focus to get on with our lives. Liz had wanted this for her very own reason, and although it was a very sad situation, it was something she chose, and we knew that she would want us to be at peace about that.

It was another Saturday night. The fire was on, it was snowing outside, the Saturday night pizza was cooking in the AGA, and beer and wine were at the ready. A perfect winter evening with the lovely thought of Christmas just being around the corner. Pete was home, and that made our evening extra special. Rufus was into a bedtime routine now and was fast asleep. We were all looking forward to the evening ahead. It was about eight o'clock when the phone rang. I would often let it just ring on a relaxing evening like that one, but for some reason, that evening I decided to pick it up. It was Avril, my niece, god-daughter, and twenty-one-year-old daughter of Mag. Her voice sounded anxious. "We have just found mummy in the car outside the house. She wasn't breathing. It doesn't look good. We are waiting for the ambulance, but she isn't breathing; I'm scared, this time it doesn't look good." Avril, the one who was usually calm and in control and who has had to ring an ambulance for her mother on numerous occasions sounded so very upset and scared that evening. I told her that I would come over straight away. When I came off the phone, Pete knew it was something serious. He just sat there, staring at the fire, motionless. He was in shock. I told him what had happened, and he said, "It's another death isn't it? Mag is dead." I said I wasn't sure but that things didn't look good. I told him that I would go over to their house and get in touch as soon as I could. I sensed that he was relieved that I was going. I knew that it was better for me to go and for him not to be confronted with another dead sister. I was in shock and went into auto pilot mode. I got in the car and started making the three mile journey through the snow to their house. All sorts of dreadful thoughts of what I was soon to find went through my head. I really just wanted to turn around and go back to what we were enjoying only fifteen minutes earlier. That wasn't an option. I knew that I had to be there to support my niece and her seventeen-year-old brother and twenty-three-year-old sister. I had always tried to be there for those children in difficult times when their mother had been ill on many occasions in their young lives, so today was no exception for me.

Their house was off the beaten track, and to reach it you had to drive down a bumpy sandy road for about 300 meters to get to their hidden cottage on the edge of the village. When I turned into their track, which was covered with snow, my heart was slowly sinking. I was getting really nervous of what I was about to find. I saw the blue light of the ambulance flashing in the distance and was relieved that it had arrived before I did. I parked the car in a neighbour's drive just a little walk away from their house where the ambulance was blocking the road. I got out of the car quickly. The cold air and eerie quietness took me by surprise. In normal circumstances walking this beauty spot in the evening snow would be blissful but on that particular evening it felt scary and sinister. My feet were making new footsteps as they were crunching in the fresh snow. As I came nearer to the house I saw Mag's car. It was swirled onto the edge of the track in a place where she would never normally park it. I had a very quick look inside and was relieved to see that she was no longer in there. The energy felt heavy and I felt fearful as I walked past her car. The next thing I saw were two of her three children, my god-daughter and her brother, shivering and crying in the dark, cold night about 20 meters away from the ambulance. They looked so lost and scared. They just stood there, motionless. I sensed relief in their eyes when they saw me arrive. I went up to them and gave them a big hug. They were cold and shivering, started crying and needed comforting. The silence was very unsettling. There was no movement in the ambulance. Their father was in the ambulance. The three of us just stood there dreading the bad news to be officially delivered. There were no words, just an agonising wait with all three of us in our own thoughts. I can't even begin to imagine what went through those children's heads. The oldest daughter arrived with her boyfriend after also having been called by Avril earlier. They had decided, like me, that this time the ambulance call was really serious and they needed to make the journey to her parental home. We all huddled up as a group and waited in the quiet of the night. Avril told me that only a few hours earlier, her mother had enjoyed putting up the Christmas decorations, something she always took great pride in during her favourite time of the year. It was an attempt to be positive after the death of her twin sister. She wanted to surprise her family when they came home from a hunting trip that evening.

After what felt an eternity, which was probably only ten minutes, their dad came out of the ambulance shaking his head. He was closely followed by one of the ambulance staff. She was dead and there was nothing they could do to save her. It was all so surreal and unreal at the same time. Nobody had been able to say goodbye to her. She was torn away from her little family just like that.

She had been to the local shop around seven o'clock on that Saturday evening which was just a two minute car drive away, to buy some goodies for their family night which she was planning to enjoy in the warm lights of the Christmas decorations. She had driven home from the shop with the evening supper in her bag but never quite made it. She managed to pull the car up to the bank and never made it into the drive. What happened in that car when she drove back from the local shop only about an hour earlier that evening? We will probably never know. What we did know for sure though was that she was dead. Two sisters died and were ripped away from their families within weeks of each other.

The ambulance drove off very slowly with her body inside. Steve and the children followed them in the car, and I went back home where I had to face my husband and tell him that his other sister had now also died. He would have to face his parents yet again and tell them that they had lost another daughter.

That evening we felt numb and somehow the time passed with us both in shock. Horrendous events were unrolling in our lives without us having any control. We continued watching TV and had wine, and life felt totally bizarre and unreal. We chose to be in total denial. How can your brain comprehend an event like that? One minute you are enjoying a nice evening and the next you suddenly, out of the blue, have to digest the news that you have lost two sisters within two months of each other. Three children and a husband were bereft from a mother and a wife, just like that.

In the weeks that followed, leading up to the funeral and Christmas we saw a lot of Maggie's husband, Steve, and the kids. We shared preparing the funeral plans and spent time together as a family, talking about and remembering Mag. Baby Rufus was a great little healer for all involved. Steve would be holding him for hours, enjoying this beautiful baby and new life that he brought us. The funeral, only days before Christmas was loving and warm and yet again surrounded by snow.

Pete's parents didn't cope at all well with the loss of their daughters. Dad very quickly deteriorated and went into depression and severe dementia literally within weeks of them dying. They couldn't cope together at home and dad was becoming very difficult and was impossible to look after. Mum had no patience with him and it was decided that it would be best for him to go to a nursing home. Mum got very lonely and all she wanted was to die herself. The year following the deaths proved to be a very difficult year all round for all involved.

DECEMBER 5, 2010
ONE YEAR AFTER MARGARET'S DEATH

The phone rang at 1:00 a.m., never a good sign. Pete was away in a hotel in London, and I was woken out of my sleep with my heart beating fast. Already at least ten horrible thoughts managed to cross my mind as I made my way to the other side of the bed where the phone was. "Can I speak to Mr. P. Leutner?" the person said.

"I'm sorry. He is not here. Can I help?"

"It's the nursing home to let you know that your father-in-law has gone to hospital with abdominal pain. He should be OK, but we thought we should let you know."

I guessed it was pretty bad for them to call at this time of the night, so I decided to give Pete a ring to tell him. He was away on location for work. He wasn't too concerned and thought it was just nursing-home practice to ring the relatives at any time of the day or night. He thought his father would probably be just fine because the caller didn't sound too serious on the phone. Pete did mention, though, that it would be ironic if his father were to die that day on December 5, a year to the day after Mag's death. We decided to presume things would be OK because a member of the nursing-home staff was with him. We decided to go back to sleep, which I managed.

At five o'clock that morning, the phone rang again. This time, it was the hospital to give us some unexpected bad news. Siegfried died that morning. Pete's family of six had been reduced to a family of three in just over one year.

Pete dealt with it privately in his own little way. He didn't talk about it too much, but he found his solace in his garden, the place that was meditative to him and where he could experience the falling of the leaves, and the beauty of new life while being productive at the same time. His growing family and work kept him busy and focussed. He showed me that everybody does their mourning and healing in their own way and at their own pace. We didn't talk about his sisters much, but I knew that when he had his time by himself in his garden they were there, in his thoughts. I felt sad for him that he hadn't been given time to say goodbye. Not even a hug or a kiss before their sudden departures from this earth.

5

Mum's Journey

It was Easter Day, and I knew when I woke up in our "English guest room," which my mother had let me design in true English style to make us feel at home, that my mother was already busy downstairs making breakfast, picking flowers, and hiding Easter eggs for the children. My mother's gift was giving. Bouquets of flowers usually picked with her own hands from her beloved garden, get-well cards with carefully thought-out words, and her precious handmade sculptures would make their way to a vast variety of houses where acquaintances, friends, or loved ones were in need of a little bit of extra thoughtful love.

When I was a young child, living on a farm surrounded by peaceful land, my mother would care for foster children from big towns during the summer holidays so that they too could have a taste of country life. When family or friends were seriously ill, my mother would look after their children for months on end. It was in her nature to care without expectations. She made a difference to many.

We had made a stopover at my mother's house for Easter on our way back home from a holiday in Germany. It had been four and a half years since my father had died. She liked our company and would go out of her way to spoil us. I wasn't wrong on that Easter morning. Every item on the breakfast table was put there with love and attention to detail, and it made us all feel special to be treated with the special "Oma touch" to it. My mother was a kind lady. Her childhood wish was to become a nurse. She was one of the oldest of ten children, and studying in her day just wasn't an option. Her entire life, she had regretted that she had never been able to fulfill that dream. Soon after she got married, she got pregnant, and four more pregnancies followed in the years to come. It was a busy time, with five children to bring up and work that needed doing on the farm. Her kitchen was forever filled with workmen and children. The sound of the cake tin opening and closing in that kitchen was familiar. I would get annoyed with her when she used to always close her eyes in church but now understand that that time must have been precious for her when she was able to have a little rest.

When we had all grown up and my father sold the farm, she started making clay sculptures. It was her relaxation and focus, and her sculptures were often associated with the happenings in her life at that time. When we, her children, started having our own children, my mother would be busy making sculptures of pregnant woman, and after that, women with babies. She never lost the desire to work in a hospital though. It wasn't until recently that she had taken on a voluntary job visiting the sick and lonely in a local hospital. She would talk to them about their worries and occasionally give them Reiki healing. She loved it and often talked to me about her experiences.

That Easter Day, just like she did on most of our visits, she would give the boys a special treat. She would take them upstairs into her meditation room, where she kept her precious stones. Her collection was impressive. She had been following courses about the stones' healing powers and shared this passion with my boys. On these occasions, when she took the boys upstairs, they would be allowed to take some of her colourful collection off her shelves. She would have them pick one and let them hold it while closing their eyes. After a few minutes, they would all share their feelings about how the stone made them feel. They were always allowed to choose one stone to take home. They loved these experiences with Oma.

Easter Day ended with a cycle ride to the chapel, where we would light a candle for the sick and loved ones who had passed on, while having some quiet reflection time.

It had been a brief but lovely short stay, and we happily drove out of the drive the next morning while hooting our horn. The children waved their little arms excitedly out of the car windows wanting to please their Oma who was happily waving back at them.

AUGUST 2011
SUMMER HOLIDAYS, FOUR MONTHS LATER

It was early August, and I was enjoying a week of blissful happiness on a family holiday with my husband and our three boys in a beautiful holiday cottage in Wales, surrounded by magical views and beautiful sunshine. We made short day trips, enjoyed sunny summer-evening barbecues, and were blessed with general quality time. It was good to have some much-needed downtime to reflect and look back over the past two difficult years. There had been joy mixed in with tiredness and difficulties in raising a young baby, but mostly there had been sadness with the sudden deaths of two sisters and a father and the grief and pain that come with sudden loss like that. We concluded that life would have to get easier now and that we were about to move into a better phase of our lives. Things couldn't get much worse than they had been for some time. I was also looking forward to having a little "me time" because Rufus was starting preschool for two mornings a week. We were looking forward to the day that Rufus would be starting nursery. Pete and I had planned a day out together when we would just relax and have coffee while reading papers, something we hadn't been able to do together for two years. It was a day to really look forward to. The Welsh holiday finished on a good note, and we drove back to Kent feeling positive.

During the last week of the summer holidays at the end of August, I took the oldest two boys to Holland for four days. I had sensed lately that having all three boys in my mother's house was getting to be a bit too much hard work for her. I was aware that she was getting older and that having all of us there, including little toddler Rufus, took its toll. The summer holidays had also affected her quite badly since my father had died. He became ill at the start of the summer holidays in 2006, and ever since my mother struggled in the summers that followed and felt lonely during those holiday months. It brought back the memories at this time of year when my father became ill. I believe that was subconsciously affecting her mood.

We spent the first few days of our Dutch visit with good friends in Rotterdam, where the boys had fun camping in their city garden, which is right in the middle of this big cosmopolitan town. After an enjoyable few days, our long-time family friend, Margo, whom we had stayed with, took us back to my mother's house. She invited Margo to join us for a coffee in her garden. My mother seemed a little low and told us that she was searching for something new in her life to distract her from her loneliness. She didn't seem to be enjoying life and was trying to embark on something new to fill a void. We suggested all sorts of potential new hobbies and activities, but nothing seemed really make her feel enthusiastic or motivated.

Looking back at that period now I see that she was anxious about something. She had a rash on her tummy that was bothering her and gave her pain. She was the kind of person who wouldn't go to the doctor willingly and tended to explain all ailments as stress or imbalance in her life. Her diet was healthy and was important to her, she never drank alcohol, and she would always eat organic food. Her self-diagnosis was that with good healthy food and vitamins, things would always get better. But during this particular week in August, fear seemed to be overpowering her mood. She did eventually go to the doctor, who diagnosed the rash to be shingles. One of her friends told her that shingles can be dangerous, and this added to her anxiety levels. She was also suffering from bad tummy aches and irregular stools. I told her to go to the doctor and get it checked out, but again she put it down to stress and nothing else. I was hoping that when life would get back into a normal routine after the summer holidays, things would settle down. She would be able to go back and enjoy her sculpting, singing lessons, and voluntary job she held in the local hospital.

On our return home to England, we were preparing to get back into our own daily routine. After six weeks of summer holidays, I was ready for the boys to go back to school again. The two oldest boys went back to school on Monday, September 5, and Rufus would start his important and life-changing first day at play school on Thursday the 8th.

I learned that my mother's tummy pains had intensified quite rapidly after we had left Holland. She was being sick a lot, and we just presumed that it was a virus of some kind.

I was pretty preoccupied with getting the kids back to school and hadn't been making my daily calls to her. When I rang her on Monday the 5th, she was still suffering from being sick and not being able to keep anything down. My siblings and I managed to convince her to go to the doctor, where blood was taken for tests. The doctor also referred her to the hospital for an outpatient appointment on Thursday to get a scan done. The pain was getting worse, but she was hanging in there because she knew that she would go to the hospital within days. She was able to eat a bit of soup but wasn't keeping much down at all, and she hadn't been able to go to the toilet for days.

When I spoke to her on Wednesday, early evening, the pain was uncontrollable. I was extremely concerned. She agreed that we should get her to a hospital as soon as possible. I rang my brother, who lives next-door to her, and told him to ring the doctor, but he was of the opinion that we should wait until the morning because she was going to the hospital for her appointment then anyway. He didn't think there was immediate danger, and it could wait a little longer. My sister-in-law, who is an ICU nurse, went to see her and she was of the opinion that something needed to be done urgently. On doctor's orders, she called an ambulance. By the time the ambulance arrived, my mother was in unbearable pain and desperate to be seen. I was hoping things would be solved, but deep down I knew that she was in real trouble. It was hard being in England because all I could do was wait for somebody to ring me. I felt powerless, and it was an agonising wait. Nobody rang.

Four hours later at about eleven o clock that night, I plucked up the courage to ring my brother, Christian, and his wife, Lizet, the ICU nurse, who had accompanied my mother in the ambulance to the hospital. He answered his phone and informed me that at that moment the doctor was talking to her, preparing her for major surgery. The doctor had felt a major obstruction in her abdomen. She was told that a good prognosis would be a polyp, and a bad prognosis would be a tumor. My heart sank, but at this stage there was hope. I told my brother to wish her good luck and that I would be thinking of her. I also told him not to call me in the night but to text me when there was more news. There was nothing I could do to make a difference in the night from such a distance. Reiki healing is not allowed during an operation. I chose to avoid any bad news during the night by leaving my phone downstairs and went to bed. I was extremely restless and didn't really sleep. I was having dark thoughts and was dreading the moment that I had to go downstairs in the morning to check the message on my phone.

SEPTEMBER 8, 2011
THE DAY OF THE DIAGNOSIS

Anxious and uncertain thoughts raced through my mind that morning. "Should I wait for the alarm to go off or go down and check the phone? What is today going to bring? Does my mum have cancer? Will Rufus's first big day at school happen? Are we going for our long-awaited morning of drinking coffee and reading papers in town? Am I going to have to travel to Holland?" I needed to find out. I couldn't postpone the truth of the result of the operation any longer because I was starting to feel sick with anxiety. I quickly pulled the duvet off my body. I sat on the edge of the bed, took a deep breath, and rapidly walked down the stairs. It was about six o'clock, an hour before the alarm was due to go off. It was one of those awful moments in my life that I will never forget, with the anxiety sky-high. I felt like a bag of nerves. The phone was lying on the table, and I knew there would be a message waiting for me.

I picked it up and saw that there was a message from my brother, Christian…I opened it and read it: "Mum came out of the operation at four o'clock this morning. She is currently in intensive care and almost didn't make it through the night. Prognosis not good."

I couldn't face the day and went back to bed and sobbed. The outcome was bad, and she has cancer. Pete was holding me whilst I was sobbing in his arms.

When the alarm went off at seven, I had to get up and get the children to school. I was only taking one step at a time at that point. The normality of daily life was welcoming. It gave me a temporary distraction from what was happening. I got the oldest two boys to school and knew I had to face more reality. I rang my sister to find out more news about my mother. She told me that things were looking very bleak. They almost lost her in the night, and the next twenty-four hours would be critical. They removed a huge malignant tumor that had gotten so big it had perforated Mum's colon. They had to take away a substantial part of her colon, which meant that if she made it through that she would have to live and deal with a colostomy bag. She was and would remain in intensive care. Bad news all around. My sister was about to go to hospital because she wanted to be there when she woke up to tell her about what had happened.

My feelings were all over the place. I didn't know what to do. Should I rush over, which wasn't easy with three young children? My husband was working the next day. I cried hysterically over the phone because of what had happened and because I couldn't make up my mind at such short notice. Everything was confusing and complicated, and I appreciated my husband taking charge and making the decisions. He decided that we would take Rufus to school and have coffee in town, as planned. He felt I needed time to let the news sink in and to organise things from a practical point of view.

First things first. Rufus was going to nursery for his first day, which was a big day for any parent and child in their lives. It's a time to let go and trust other people to look after your baby—a new phase in your life and theirs. Rufus was happy to go, but when we left, he screamed. I knew he was well prepared for school, and I had told him that Mummy would leave but that Mummy would come back. I also knew he was in good hands of some special ladies who had also looked after my other two boys when they were at preschool age. I needed some time away from him to take in the fact that my mother was in intensive care and that I may never see her alive again. It was all surreal, and my senses felt numbed.

Pete and I were walking hand in hand through town and chose a place to have coffee. We were finally sitting down to enjoy this moment we had been looking forward to, but the reality was a million miles away from a relaxing morning in town that we had envisaged. Where do you start? I suppose you might find it strange that I hadn't already got onto the plane to see my mother. Thinking back, I think it is strange, too, but the reality was that I needed my nearest and dearest to process this, and I'm not sure I would have been safe driving to Holland. Then again, I could have gone on the train, but I just couldn't pull myself away from the security of home and was scared of facing the reality in Holland. I was protecting myself in a funny sort of way. I was able to do this because I knew my mother was in good hands with my brothers and sister by her side. I didn't feel it would make much of a difference to her if I had been there on that particular day. If she had died on that day, I would have been able to live with that because of the experience I had had with my father, who had told me that I belonged with my family in England. I had to be there to pick up Rufus from his first day at school.

Pete made a call to work. I think his boss was shocked to hear about our news, knowing how much grief the family had already been through. He was sympathetic and gave him time off to deal with whatever needed dealing with. We didn't think she would live very long and felt it was right that he was given time to deal with this. After that phone call to his work, in theory, I was free to go to Holland. But first, I wanted to pick up my baby from his nursery school. How could I not pick him up after his first day? So we stayed in town all morning, making phone calls and processing in my head what had happened in the past twenty-four hours.

I decided to go to Holland on my own because Mum was in intensive care, and the last thing anybody wanted there was a two-year-old toddler.

My sister had been with her all day, waiting for her to wake up to tell her the bad news. When I spoke to my sister that evening, she told me that Mum was still unconscious. It had been hard for her to sit with my mother all day, but I was so grateful that she had. I told her I would come the following day, which was also my sister's birthday, but I felt an awful reluctance. I did not want to go. I just couldn't face leaving all my children, even though their dad was at home. I feared making the journey on my own. I have had separation anxiety ever since I had my own children and have a fear of losing them when I leave them. I detest the fact that I feel this way, but I just can't help it. I don't have any control over it. I told my sister of these issues, and she said I should bring Rufus because the other children could look after him. So in the end, I took my oldest and my youngest sons. The middle boy, Henry, decided to stay with his dad. Once I made this decision, I was good to go. I was apprehensive to see my mother in intensive care but knew deep down that once I got there, I would be OK. I believe that facing your fears helps you get over them. Another anxious and restless night followed.

SEPTEMBER 9
ONE DAY AFTER THE DIAGNOSIS

Once packed and on our way, I was able to make some mental preparation for the moment I was going to see my mother that afternoon. The situation was still critical. Most of my five hour journey was overshadowed by thoughts about losing her and how life would be without her. Music would trigger memories, and tears were rolling down my cheeks on an almost permanent basis. My children were keeping it real, and I was glad I had chosen to take them with me. Our unconditional love for each other kept me going strong. As we got closer to Holland, I was getting more and more nervous. My sister and I had decided that I would come to her house before visiting our mother together, which meant passing the hospital in which she was lying, located next to the motorway. It was a strange feeling, passing it, knowing my mother was wired up to life-saving equipment. I just couldn't bear the thought of walking up to her bed in intensive care on my own, and I wasn't allowing myself to feel guilty about it. My sister would be holding my hand as we walked into that unfamiliar place of beeping lights where my mother was wired up to keep her alive.

Twenty minutes after passing the hospital, we arrived at my sister's house. We embraced and cried. I felt sorry for her as it was her birthday and she had spent most of the day holding my mother's hand in intensive care, waiting for her to wake up to break the devastating news. She never woke up that day.

We shared our emotions and the fact that we would lose our mother to cancer over a contrasting piece of birthday cake. It felt right to celebrate her birthday, and eating cake seemed an appropriate way to do it. I was dreading the trip to the hospital to see my unconscious mother in all the pain she was in, while kept asleep with sedating morphine. I so wished for her to be at my sister's house to share some birthday cake with us.

After an hour or so, we decided to make our way to the hospital. The short car journey seemed to last an eternity, and I was scared of how I would find her. My sister was aware of my anxiety and managed to calm me a little bit. I knew that once I had made contact with my mother I would be calm, but working myself up to that moment was agonisingly difficult. As we parked at the side of the hospital, a flood of memories came back from when my father was in the very same hospital almost five years earlier to the day. Why did we have to go through this painful journey again?

The big sliding doors at the entrance slid open, and we walked into what looked like a big shopping centre filled with cafes, shops, and buzz. We could almost imagine once again that we were on holiday until realising that the people in white coats were doctors and nurses and that the people in wheelchairs were sick patients. It soon took me back to the harsh reality.

We entered the same lift as we did when my father had been there. So many previous emotions and thoughts came flooding back but didn't distract me from the fact that soon I would set foot in intensive care.

More sliding doors followed. My sister took hold of my hand, so I knew we were getting close. She talked me through the rooms in the long corridor and told me it wasn't until we got to the last room on the right that we would get there. Apart from "beep" noises, there was an eerie quietness on the ward. Finally we reached the last door on the right, and my grip on my sister's hand became firmer and firmer. We looked at each other, and I took a deep breath. She pulled me along gently. We entered a big room with lots of beeping machinery and my mum looking tiny as she lay asleep in a big bed in the middle of the room. I went up to the bed to look at her and all the attached wires and tried to be brave and strong. I took her hand and said, "Hi, Mum. I'm here." She drifted out of her "sleep," slightly squeezed my hand, and said, "I'm glad you are here." Then she drifted back off.

We just stood there, my sister and myself, each on one side of my mother, just talking about her and holding her hands. I remember my sister saying, "Feel how cold her hands already are." I was aware that these might well be the final moments I would have with my mother. It was like time stood still for a little while. Nothing existed but the three of us in that space without time. The sound of the bleeps were taking on a meditative function while we stood quietly, holding her cold hands and surrounding her with love from her two daughters.

My mother's mouth was very dry, and my sister had learned the ropes of intensive care in the previous days. She kept her mouth damp with little sticks that she dropped into water. I just stood there and felt quite powerless, not knowing how to be useful. I didn't enjoy being there, and I could tell my mother was in pain. She made noises that appeared painful. I felt torn and found it difficult to be with her in this deeply distressing state. I just wanted to run back out of the room. My whole life, I had never been good when pets or animals became ill or died. I remember my goldfishes dying and being petrified just to walk past their bowl, with the bendy-looking fish floating at the top. Now I had to face this fear with my own mother. It was a much easier option to go back to my sister's house, where my children were happily playing. While holding her hands, I wondered if her pale hands really were getting colder. Those thoughts were quite torturing, and I was glad when my sister finally said, "Let's go home" after an hour or so of visiting. I kissed her goodbye and told her I would be back in the morning.

That night, the boys and I slept under my sister's skylight. There was a thunderstorm. Lying there looking up at the heavens, I wondered why our lives had been hit by yet more storms.

SEPTEMBER 10
TWO DAYS AFTER THE DIAGNOSIS

We were all up quite early. We hadn't had any news during the night, so no news was good news we thought.

I called the hospital and they gave us good news. Mum had been moved away from intensive care in the night and onto the oncology ward. The surgeon had asked to have a meeting with the family at eleven o'clock which my sister and I would attend.

Somehow things felt a bit lighter and less immediate now she had moved from ICU, but of course the fact that my mother was to die because of terminal cancer remained, but our goalposts were changing on a daily basis. So far, today was a good start.

We found her in her own room, with a lovely view, one that took me back to the time when my father was in the same ward.

She was much more awake and talkative but still in a lot of pain. The wires were still attached and pulled up her nostrils, giving her a strange appearance. She was visibly pleased to see us and told us of a disturbed night when she was moved onto the ward. It was very difficult to have a decent conversation because of her discomfort. We asked the nurse for some extra morphine so she would be able to focus on the meeting with the surgeon who was going to break the bad news to her. By the time he came she appeared more comfortable. I was grateful to him that he managed to save her during that crucial night two days ago. He was a big strong man and told us about the operation and how she almost died under his hands. There was a massive tumor blocking her small intestines which he had removed, but he also told us that the tumor had spread all over her body, including the liver and blood. He didn't know where the cancer originated, either the intestines or the pancreas. He would get this tested. Her colon was perforated, hence the immediate danger. The next week would still be critical. He told us that there was no hope and that the cancer *would* win the battle and he estimated that she would still have weeks, possibly months to live. I noticed my mother quietly taking all this in.

The surgeon's news was a lot to take in for us, too. I can't even begin to think of how my mother must have felt. She was quiet but the first thing she said after he had gone was "Miracles do happen." A good sign I thought, she won't give into it easily and why can't there be hope? She was right, miracles do happen.

Although the news was bad she was still here with us and appeared to get better by the day. So very rapidly our goalposts changed and we were very much just living in the moment, enjoying being with her.

You have to deal with what is thrown at you on your path of life. I believe that human beings have all been given a coping force that kicks in in times of troubles.

The same coping force kicked in with my mother. She had decided there and then that she was going to fight this cancer whatever it took. Our return to England was imminent and with it came the realisation that she may never see my children again. Even though she was still very weak she wanted to see the children before we left for England. We would be back with the children later that day after she had a rest.

The road from my sister's house to the hospital and back was already becoming familiar. It's amazing how quickly I also clicked into the familiarity of being there with my sick mother and being able to care for her. So glad I was staying with my sister so we could share this difficult and unusual time. The children, including my sister's two came with us to hospital later on. We decided to take it in turn with our own children in seeing her. Two-year-old Rufus, thirteen-year-old Luke and myself went in first. It was refreshing to have Rufus skipping along the hospital corridors. A toddler really does lighten the load in some difficult situations. I could tell that Luke was nervous of how to find his grandmother and he too enjoyed having his care free and happy little brother there. High hopes that she would be pain free and bright.

We all went quiet as mice when we entered the cancer ward while we were walking towards her room. I was preparing my children, just as my sister prepared me, which seemed to comfort them.

When we walked into her room she gave us the most beautiful beaming smile. It was a lovely and comforting feeling to see her like that. Rufus was of course happy to see her until he noticed all the wires which scared him. Instead of sitting on the bed with her he just hid away on my shoulders. I decided to put him on the wide ledge of the big window with the beautiful view where he was happy walking along and looking at all the busyness of "normal" life that seemed to be going on out there while mum visibly enjoyed watching him do just that. Seeing Rufus gave her hope and will power to fight and be positive. The presence of the children did her the world of good. Luke was just hovering at the end of the bed, finding it difficult to make eye contact with his grandmother and struggled with the situation they were both in. My mum always had treated him a bit special because all his life he had suffered from severe eczema. It was hard for him to see her as she was, but I expect it was also a relief to him to see her smile and talk. She called him to the side of her bed and held his hand and made him look into her eyes and told him that miracles do happen and that she had read about a person in Italy who had only been given weeks to live due to cancer and who had conquered the disease and was now happy and well. The fact that she passed on her hope to my teenage son was comforting to him. She could have chosen to make it a final emotional goodbye, but I respected her for the choice of hope she gave him instead.

Despite the message of hope the remaining ten minutes were filled with emotions and tears of release. I told her that I would come back the next morning on my own before returning to England. I felt quite elated when walking away from the ward that afternoon and relieved that my mum's emotional state was strong. There was hope for something worthwhile in our future together with our mother and grandmother.

The evening that followed with my sister was again emotional. It was all still such a shock that we would be losing her. The realisation kept popping up all through the day with the tears that went with this devastating emotion. I was feeling enlightened though by my mother's attitude and this somehow gave me some more space in my head. I was dreading saying my goodbyes the next day and there were slight feelings of guilt that perhaps I should be staying here until she died, after all the doctor only expected her to live weeks, perhaps months. But with one child still at home in England, school to attend and a husband travelling for work a lot of the time this wasn't an option so the reality called me back home.

THREE DAYS AFTER THE DIAGNOSIS

The next morning I was very aware that it could well be the last time that I would ever see my mother alive. Before going to visit her I went back to my mother's place to pick up some of her personal belongings. It really hit me when I walked into her house how our lives had been turned upside down. Seeing all the signs of normality such as leftover food in the fridge, dressing gown hanging in the bathroom, and bits of her recent writing on a piece of paper made it all come home to me. Was all this really happening? It suddenly seemed like a bad nightmare. Surely I would wake up soon, and my mum would be walking through that door.

I packed a nice box to take to the hospital with me. In it I placed one of her angel sculptures, a picture of my dad, some flowers, a nice scarf, some nice-smelling lotions, and a vase to make her room look homely and cosy. I was becoming more and more anxious and nervous about going while I was making the fifteen-minute journey from my mother's house to the hospital. This was the first time I would visit her alone since she fell ill. I felt annoyed with myself that I was anxious about seeing my own mother. When I arrived at the hospital, I plucked up the courage to get out of the car and clamped my fingers onto the box of things I had taken for her. I was totally in my own zone and unaware of anything going on around me. It felt like I was a character in a film to whom something scary was just about to happen. I wanted it over and done with. Saying farewell to your own mother and knowing it could be forever must be one of the worst emotional goodbyes that any human would ever have to encounter. I entered the oncology ward and picked up my pace, knowing that once I was with her, I would be OK and cope. Why is it that the anticipation of a difficult task is usually a lot worse than the reality?

As I entered her room, she was clearly waiting for me to arrive, pain under control and sitting upright in her bed. She gave me a big smile, and I could tell that she was aware of why I had come. I sat next to her, holding her hand, and started to cry. I knew I had to do the "I love you bit." Otherwise, I may later regret it. I also knew I had to tell her that it was OK for her to die and that I would be able to cope without her. "I love you, Mum," I said.

She replied, "I know." She was of the older generation who didn't say "I love you" easily. She had always struggled to express her emotions. I asked her, "Do you love me, too, Mum?"

She answered a bit crossly, "Of course I love you. What a silly question to ask!" It was all a little bit awkward, but I was glad I got the "I love you" conversation out of the way. When you haven't been brought up that way, even though you know you're loved unconditionally by your parents and you love them unconditionally, it doesn't come very naturally to say these things.

A female priest walked into the room, a welcome interruption to the awkwardness we both felt at the time. She asked if we wanted to receive communion. I told her my mother was really, really ill and hadn't been given long to live, and perhaps she could come and spend some time to talk with us. While she was there, I opened the box I had filled up with things for my mum and took out the angel sculpture she made to show to the priest. I could see the enjoyment on my mother's face when she was able to talk about her sculpture and her love for sculpting. She didn't want to be confronted about her illness; instead, she wanted to talk about normal day-to-day things. At the end of her visit, the priest gave us both an emotional blessing, a very welcoming gesture that felt very appropriate in those moments of us being together.

After the priest had gone, it was soon time for us to say our goodbyes. I didn't allow myself to dwell on the fact that it could be the last time I would ever see her. Instead, I was going to presume that I would see her again soon. I had already planned in my head that I would have to come back soon to spend more time with her. I gave her a big hug, held her hand, and said goodbye. I sensed that she also decided to do the same thing, presuming we would see each other again really soon. Perhaps it was a coping mechanism kicking in, but I also think that subconsciously we knew we would be together again. When the time came to leave, we held eye contact a lot longer than usual. In those few seconds of looking into each other's eyes, I felt a deep, deep connection with her that I hadn't felt in that way before. In those few seconds, I felt the unconditional love of a mother for her child, and I felt my unconditional love for my mother. Our future together was very much in doubt.

Walking out of her room, I had the urge to look at her one more time and turned around. I saw her looking at me walking away from her, back to England, where I had to go to be a mother to my own children. She waved and smiled at me, and a nurse walked in and handed her a cup of soup, which comforted me. She wasn't ready to give in to this cancer just yet.

Walking out of the hospital doors back towards "normal life," my mobile phone made a text message sound, drawing me back into life outside the hospital. A kind friend texted, "Thinking of you at this difficult time." Her timing couldn't have been more appropriate. There were many friends out there for me, and receiving texts like that were so comforting.

I drove back to my mother's house, where my sister and brothers had decided to gather with all their children, as they had done every Sunday before my mother fell ill. They were making the most of it while the house was still there. My boys were there, too, playing with their cousins. I made time for a quick coffee before we had to set off for England.

Walking into my mum's house was already feeling so different than it ever had before. Finding the rest of the family sitting there in quietness and anticipation of what I had to say about what may have been my last meeting with our mother was also a strange experience.

They were surprised that I felt positive and that I was optimistic and didn't feel it was the last time I had spent time with her. I told them about my visit to the hospital and how I felt that she was ready to fight the cancer, how I still believed that we had time to make more memories. I noticed everybody relaxed a little, knowing that at that moment things were possibly on the up rather than down and that we were able to perhaps move some goalposts.

We said our goodbyes, and my two boys and I headed back to our home on the long drive to England.

It felt so nice to be back home with my own little family unit complete. Knowing I would be back in Holland ten days later gave me some inner calm during the days at home in England.

Friends were kind to me when I came home, offering help with cooking and picking up the children. That was touching, but the best therapy for me was to do all of my everyday tasks myself. Those routines of daily life kept me going strong, focused and distracted.

One thing that upset me was seeing mums and daughters together. Their intimate chats and familiarity with each other would bring tears to my eyes. It made me realise that it was likely I would never be able to have a healthy and taken-for-granted mother-daughter connection with my own mother again.

My mother decided and told the doctors very clearly that she wanted no more treatment and interference. She was of the opinion that the taking of blood and temperature every few hours and the disturbance this caused during the nights and periods of rest was not necessary. She felt it was doing her more harm than good, so she decided to let nature take its course. She was becoming uncomfortable due to breathlessness caused by fluid on her lungs, and until this fluid lessened and she started passing urine again, her condition continued to be critical. As the noninterference days went on, nature took its course for the positive, and she was slowly getting stronger. Moving from ICU into a room of her own was a major positive step. Only about a week later, she was transferred into a ward with three other patients. Even though she was told what her destiny would be and that her cancer was terminal, she continued talking about a miracle and was focusing on getting home. She had a will to live, and a fighting spirit was emerging, which must have been helping the healing process.

The next goal for her was to get home. On the evening when she was ripped away in excruciating pain from her house and urgently transported in the ambulance, she certainly hadn't planned that to be the last time she would leave her house. Her attitude was that if she was going to have to die, she would want to do so at home, just like my dad had done before her.

Coming home in the condition she was in was not straightforward, though, and a lot had to be organised before she would be able to come back to the home she loved so much. She was still gravely ill. Full-time nursing care and equipment such as beds, commodes, medication, plus doctors' visits had to be put in place before the all-important day of coming home could become a reality. In Holland, terminally ill people get considerable funding from the state, which often makes it possible for them to die at home. After much organising and planning, we were given the date of Monday, September 19 for the big homecoming day. It would coincide with my coming back home from England.

MONDAY, SEPTEMBER 19, 2011
ELEVEN DAYS AFTER THE DIAGNOSIS, COMING HOME

It was a comforting thought that both my mother and I were making the journey from such different places on the same day to a place we both called home and that we would be able to enjoy time together without immediate danger and added anxiety of her dying. She was, for now, still recovering from the major surgery and was getting stronger as time went on. It was mentally easier for me, knowing my mother was not in immediate danger, to leave my children in England with their father. I was also looking forward to taking the more relaxing route by train to Brussels. It was a luxury for me to be there for my mother 100 percent without any children causing distraction. Pete and the boys would come over to pick me up on a day trip a couple of days later, and my friend, Ria, would pick me up from a local Belgium train station not too far from my mother's house. Ria and I grew up together, and she had been a very good friend since we were just four years old. She still lives in the area I grew up in, and she proved to be an amazing support for me when my parents were ill, in every sense. She was always a true friend, calling me, offering to help in any way she could. As the train entered the little station of Turnhout, Ria was there waving from the platform, sharing some of my journey with me. We embraced, and I appreciated her being there for me. As we walked to her car, I suddenly realised that my suitcase was missing. I soon remembered that I left it behind in a coffee shop at Brussels train station, a whole hour away on the train. It was a real upset that I could have done without. It was a strong indicator that my mind was preoccupied with distractions during my journey. Ria told me not to worry about it; she would arrange to get it back somehow. She drove me back to her house for some lunch, which gave me a chance to get over the suitcase scenario and enabled me to emotionally prepare myself to go and see my mother. My sister-in-law, Lizet, a nurse, would settle her into her newly adapted home environment. I chose to join her once she was comfortable and acclimated to her new home surroundings. Lunch at Ria's home was a nice transition for me. There was always this anticipation and anxiety because I hadn't been there for a while. For some reason, every time I returned, it was hard to enter back into the situation that was happening at home. Every time, though, I would also know that as soon as I set foot in the door and saw her, all would be just fine. I think a situation often looks worse from the outside, but once you step into it, everything becomes a part of everyday life. It's a matter of embracing and facing it so that fear will go away.

Once Ria and I were having lunch, it didn't take long before I got twitchy and wanted to go and see my mum. We finished our lunch promptly, and Ria took me to the house. My heart was beating fast as we were making the five-minute drive. I was annoyed with myself for feeling anxious yet again, but there was no way of controlling it. I just went with it. Ria dropped me off outside the house. We agreed that it may be too tiring for my mother if she came, too. As I walked up the drive, I thought how amazingly lucky we were that she had come home. She almost died only weeks earlier, when I walked into the house then, that Sunday after saying goodbye to her in the hospital. It was emotional because I realised that our mother might never be there to welcome us again. Yet here we were only weeks later, and she would be in the house to welcome me.

I was nervous to see her and had to pluck up the courage to open the door, walk through the hallway, and then through the kitchen before entering the lounge. One more door. I knew that my anxiety of seeing her again would disappear as soon as our eyes had made contact. I opened the door into the lounge. There she was, lying in a huge hospital bed by the window in the very same place as my dad had been lying in the final months of his life. A flash of this memory of my father lying there in agony soon vanished when my mother's beaming smile made that negative thought disappear as quickly as it appeared. I was astonished at how well she looked, and the true joy in her face made it a very happy and special homecoming. I gave her a big hug and was delighted to share this momentous day of her homecoming with her. This was what she had longed and fought for during those weeks in the hospital. All the uncertainty about the awful fact that she might never come home and that she could have died in a hospital, a place she developed a phobia for after her sister died there twenty years earlier, could be put behind her. She certainly gave the impression that she wasn't going to go back to the hospital again and that she was here to stay...until the end. We were going to treat each day as if it was a little lifetime in itself and make the most of the unknown period of gifted time we had left. We as her family would support her during this journey with unconditional love. Today was the start of a new journey for all of us. Today was a happy day.

The grandchildren had made her a life-sized poster with a lovely picture of her on it that read "Welcome Home, Oma." The cards and flowers she had received were all nicely arranged around the house. She described her homecoming that day as "paradise, heaven on earth." She was truly happy, and I don't think I had ever seen her in such a euphoric way before. It was a joy to share that memorable day with her. It was a light experience among the dark days we had endured in the weeks before.

Later on that afternoon, we were expecting one of the six new nurses who would be looking after her twenty-four hours a day. The nurse was Maria. She must have been around sixty years old. There was an instant "click" between my mother and Maria. The fact that she was called Maria amused my mother. She had been trying a make a sculpture called Maria that she just couldn't seem to get the way she wanted. The fact that Maria then appeared in her life in body explained it all. She was given the real thing! Almost as soon as Maria had settled in, she started making rules that would benefit my mother. The first thing she introduced was visiting hours. She said it was important that she had her daily resting periods, and it was decided that between noon and 2:00 p.m. and between 5:00 p.m. and 7:00 p.m., nobody was to call in or phone. This would include us, her children and grandchildren. This was a fantastic idea because she would now be able to rest peacefully without any disturbance during those particular hours. She also changed the lounge around so that instead of my mum having to look backward to people sitting on the sofa, she made the chairs face her bed. It was a simple bit of brilliance. It turned out that all the nurses, about six of them rotating in twenty-four-hour shifts, all had their own special qualities. While one might be good at household chores, the other one would be a good listener. Others had the qualifications of Reiki and reflexology, which were also useful to my mother's condition. There was a good balance of lovely and talented ladies who cared for my mother very well. My mother did not want the children to be responsible for her care, after what she went through with my father. Looking after a gravely sick person with whom you have a close relationship is extremely hard, both mentally and physically. She felt it was worth the extra money just to make the time with her children a quality experience rather than her being a burden.

That evening, some of the grandchildren came to see her. Everybody was visibly happy to have her back home. That night, we all went to bed contented, calm, and happy. For me it was truly special that I was back visiting my mother in her house. The fact that there was twenty-four-hour care and somebody there with her even at night made it a relaxing time for me. I had a lovely hot bath and went to bed, looking forward to spending time with my mum for the next three days.

It was that day that my mother posted on her blog for the first time. We had started this blog when she first fell ill to keep friends and family updated, and so far it had been her children updating it. But today she wanted to write something. I will continue placing her posts during her journey in this book. I know she would have loved her blog posts to be shared with you, the reader. She knew that I was planning to write a book about my losses and she wanted to make a little difference and give some insight into what it is like to live with terminal cancer.

A Message from Toos

Dear friends, dear family, and lovely people who have sent meaningful cards and messages via this blog: it is an overwhelming feeling to get all your attention. Your words, messages, and flowers are so very healing for me and received with love.

Today I finally came home again, and it feels like paradise, like heaven on earth. I hope to be able to enjoy my own little haven for some time to come.

SEPTEMBER 20
TWELVE DAYS AFTER THE DIAGNOSIS
I woke up that morning and felt slight apprehension of how her first night had been. It was a luxury for me to be able to have a bath and get ready in peace, something I could only dream of at home as a

mother with three growing boys. When I came down that morning, Maria was bathing my mother and taking care of her needs. All I had to do was make myself some breakfast to enjoy.

During the emergency operation two weeks earlier, she had been fitted with a colostomy bag. While she was recovering from the major surgery, it was more of an insignificance compared to the major health issues that were going on at the time. This stoma was now becoming more of a significant problem, though, and it proved quite complex to get the right attachment to the new opening that was made during surgery. Sometimes it leaked or didn't fit properly. It was a piece of "new body" that had to be accepted both by body and person. Suddenly, after seventy-five years of normal stools, it is a mental transformation to accept the new way of how her body had to function. She had had a leak the previous night that affected her mood that morning. My mother was a proud woman who always took great care of herself. Finding herself lying in poo that morning was embarrassing and humiliating for her. I would have found that extremely difficult to have had to deal with, and this is where the nursing care at home was so wonderful. They were able to give her a positive experience so that she kept her dignity, which was just as important as her medical care. They dealt with it brilliantly. Maria washed her and spoke positive words and then got her ready for the day to come, smelling clean and looking beautiful again.

I spent a happy day with her. The excitement of being home still brought her intense happiness. The fact that we were together again brought us both much delight. Knowing that you have limited time together makes you embrace the time you do have, and you live it intensely. Her pain was controlled with little pipes of morphine. Being pain-free and able to just be together with the nurses taking care of the nursing, the food, and washing left us to enjoy the little things that mattered.

In the back of my mind, though, was a shadow slowly closing in with the sadness that I would have to say goodbye again the next day.

SEPTEMBER 21
THIRTEEN DAYS AFTER THE DIAGNOSIS

The night hadn't been pain-free, and I could read the pain in her face when I came down. Thinking of the awful pain my father had to endure during his journey with cancer, it suddenly made me realise that times ahead were going to be tough. But with the love of our family and friends, we would somehow be able get through it. If no pain were involved, the journey to death would be so much easier, although somebody told me once that pain brings you closer to God. I suspected that time would also come for my mother. For now, though, she was able to control it with small doses of morphine and was able to make the most of the time she had left.

That morning, we were yet again both aware of the fact that it could possibly be our last-ever day together. Yet again, knowing it could be our final hours together made us make the most of our time. We tried to escape the reality and chose to reminisce about the past while looking at old photographs. One of her specialities was taking photographs that she lovingly put into every child's own individual photo albums and kept for every one of us siblings. Photos are precious, and they were evoking nice memories. It felt like stepping back into the "pain-free, precancer" era for us. Although we enjoyed stepping back, it must also have been difficult for her to see some of the pictures, realising that "the before the cancer time" would never come back. Her GP came in halfway through us looking at the photo albums and joined us in our conversation. Then we went on to discuss medical matters and issues, such as pain management. Before she got ill, my mother would rarely reach for painkillers, not even one paracetamol, so his suggestion of upping her morphine was a lot for her to take in, even though he said the dose was still relatively small. The GP's visit generally was the highlight of her day. The emotional support of her doctor was crucial. He would speak to her with sensitivity and made her feel as if she was heard and involved her in decisions. He gave her a real important positive patient experience.

It was during this visit from the doctor when my boys came running in, having come all the way from England, and gave me a huge big hug. It felt like a breath of fresh air had come sweeping into the house— especially little two-year-old Rufus with his huge smile gave my mum a lot of joy. After the initial entry and excitement of seeing their mummy and Oma, the older boys became shy and were unsure how to handle the situation. We had taken them out of school for the day to make the journey to Holland, thinking it may be their last opportunity to see their grandmother. The older two boys had become introverted about the fact that she was going to die. They had already had to deal with so many family deaths in the previous years. They had chosen not to talk about the subject. I did feel that coming over to Holland and seeing her smile and be positive would help them deal with it. The deaths of their aunties and English grandfather were so sudden, they couldn't really comprehend them, but my mother's case was different. I felt that it was important because they had the opportunity and time to visit her. It would help them in their grief and acceptance of what was happening to her and themselves.

The boys sat on the sofa calmly. They only had a couple of hours with her before we all had to make the journey back to England. My mother asked Rufus to come and sit on the bed with her, which he did for a long time. She had prepared a gift for him, a little musical box that she wanted to give him. He was so excited and accepted it with pure joy. He opened it, and in it was a rose quartz heart for him. He gave it to her, and she pressed the heart against her heart and gave it back to him. He opened the box, and we all enjoyed the music that oozed out of it. Then he put the stone back in the box. Soon after that, he opened the box again, took out the heart, and gave it to her. This exchange of love and hearts and the blowing of kisses went on for about ten minutes. They were both so alive and so happy and totally in the moment. Pete was watching them with tears rolling down his cheeks. The realisation that our youngest child may never experience that kind of joy with his grandmother again really touched him. Time seemed to stand still in this moment of extremes, which was making us feel joyous and sad at the same time.

Our young boy's purity had caused a look of pure joy for life in my mother, and she asked to sit outside in her garden for the first time since she got home from hospital. It was a beautiful sunny day, and we wrapped her up warm, sat her in her wheelchair, and watched her happy face bathing in the sunshine, breathing in the air she knew so well. She watched my boys play in the much-loved and climbed-in walnut tree in the garden. It was like a kind of euphoria had come over her.

Those beautiful hours spent with my boys, my husband, and my mother flew by, and the time to say goodbye came too soon. I let the boys do their goodbyes first. They all gave her big, heartfelt hugs, hugs that I was only accustomed to when hugging my children or husband and that I found difficult to give to my mother. I made a quick decision that I would presume that I was going to see her soon again, so I gave her a little hug and told her I would be back soon. Then I left, keeping it as casual as I could possibly get away with.

While driving away from the house, my tears were emerging, but deep down I really believed I was going to see her again.

My life back in England was unsettled, and any sense of inner peace was scarce. I didn't know if I was coming or going. I had barely got home before I had to plan when I would go back. There was no escaping from the harsh reality that my mother was dying. The packing and unpacking of suitcases and the not being able to plan anything in my life was exhausting and frustrating. Everything that was put on the calendar had a question mark attached to it, and I wasn't sure how long I could keep this up. I never really felt alone in all this, though, and the support of friends around me helped.

Weblog: September 23
Fifteen Days after the Diagnosis–Toos

Hi, everyone,

I have a special hospital bed in the lounge. I can see many of my local friends and villagers walk by. They often wave. I have to admit that I'm quite jealous of them. There is nothing that I would want more than to go for a walk with not a care in the world. I would never take good health for granted again.

Everyone, thank you for the many loving messages. I love looking at the bouquets of flowers that I have been given that brighten up my home and enjoy having visitors, but please keep them short and call before your visit. I do get tired very quickly.

Toos

My mother's recovery from the operation continued, and she was visibly getting stronger. What was going on invisibly was another matter on which we chose not to focus. Only a few days after I said goodbye to her, she started taking little walks through the garden while holding somebody's arm and getting up and about to potter in the house a little. While I was there, she was still very much bedbound, but she was determined to strengthen her leg muscles and give them exercise. She was also able to enjoy receiving special care and love from family and friends more. My mother was a giving person, and initially it was difficult for her to embrace all the attention without being able to give back, so this receiving was a real lesson she had to learn in this final phase of her life. Usually it was she who would visit the sick and needy, but now she was the sick and needy. I'm convinced that people were thrilled to give her something back, and it was lovely to see her be so very spoiled. Her favourite part of the day was the arrival of the postman. He delivered cards and gifts, each containing lovely and caring wishes. She was able to say thank you. By saying thank you, she acknowledged that she had received. Through all this love and attention that people so much wanted to give her, she discovered that she was worthwhile. As the weeks went on, a transformation took place; she was becoming really happy. Her face was shining again as she was accomplishing more wishes. She certainly didn't want life to just slip away through her fingers. Instead, she took precious time to feed her soul.

While my mother was enjoying and embracing her life at home, it certainly made life in England so much easier for me, too. While she was happy, I could be, too.

September 26
Happy days

Hi, everyone,

The pain that was due to the major surgery is subsiding. This obviously makes me feel a lot better also because I am enjoying food again.

In the last few days, I have been well enough to take short walks in the garden and enjoyed the fresh air while the sun was beaming onto my face. It does me a world of good to be outside.

I am surrounded and cared for by some very fine nurses who give me a lot of attention.

Toos

OCTOBER 10
ONE MONTH AFTER THE DIAGNOSIS

WE HAVE TURNED A GOOD CORNER

I had a bad night's sleep due to clock watching! Leaving on the 5:50 a.m. shuttle made it an early start. I kissed my boys goodbye while they were still sleeping. Once in the car, I focussed on where I was going and listened to the music on the radio that would, as always, stir up my emotions and trigger memories. Things were still going really well with my mother. The pain seemed to be under control, and my intention for the visit was to have quality time with her. Driving through the Belgium countryside before reaching the Dutch border, seeing the sun come up on the flat land with its many churches and knotted trees, wasn't all that bad. I was getting so used to this journey and was starting to appreciate the beauty of the Belgian countryside. Having to deal with a sick and ageing parent was a challenge, but it is also part of life's natural cycle.

When I arrived after the three-hour drive, it was so easy to open the door to the house. This time, things were going well. My mother sat in a chair looking beautiful and radiant. Like me, she was looking forward to spending quality time together. Because I had no children with me, it felt like I had all the time in the world for her. More people would be visiting her now because she was more up to it. Although this was never a said thing, I sensed that many friends and some family came to say their farewells. I enjoyed the visitors, many of them old family friends and family I hadn't seen for a long time, but I did make sure they didn't outstay their welcome. Long chats would make Mum feel tired. From a purely selfish point of view, I also wanted to have my mum to myself. Her resting periods were such a wonderful idea because she knew she wouldn't be disturbed at those times, and she could really relax and often had a good little sleep. The nurses would guard the door so nobody would go in or out during those times.

In the afternoon, I took my mother out into the village in a wheel-chair. People were delighted to see her, and all went out of their way to have a little chat. Many of these villagers talked about their memo-ries that involved my mother, which they had enjoyed with her in their lifetimes. My mum made an interesting observation about how her life was being retold to her by different people in different sections. I sup-pose when you know that somebody is dying, it evokes your memories that you have with them.

We bumped into Ria's mother, who invited us for coffee. It was the first time my mum had visited anybody since the operation. We were chatting away, and everything felt normal—my mum and me on an afternoon out. The sense of normality felt special, and doing these normal things was something that I had thought would never happen again one month earlier. All I saw then was mothers and daughters in town together having a good time. Never did I think that I would be lucky enough to ever be going out with my mum for quality mother-daughter time. So there you go…never say never! You don't know what is around the corner. This particular corner we had recently turned was a good one. There was a realisation that all had not gone and that life together was to be enjoyed while we still could.

This day had done her a world of good, and I think for her, too there was the realisation that if you live in the moment, life can still be good. In previous weeks, pain had stood in the way of enjoyment. But on this particular day, it was under control, and it made our visit special and easy.

That evening, we decided to invite her four sisters for coffee the next morning.

OCTOBER 11
CELEBRATION CAKE

Most mornings while visiting my mother, I would come down the stairs with slight hesitation, not knowing how the night had been and how she was feeling that day. The previous day had been amazing. Perhaps things had changed again? Could we be so lucky to get another nice day just like the previous one?

She was dressed and yet again looked beautiful and serene. She asked me to go to the bakery and buy the best cakes in the shop, filled with cream. She wanted to celebrate togetherness with her sisters and me.

Also on the shopping list were crystal hearts that she wanted to give to her four sisters. It was her way of unifying the sisters with a symbol of love. My aunts arrived, all slightly hesitant, not knowing how she would be. As soon as they saw her with this happy energy surrounding her, they were immediately put at ease. The morning was filled with laughter and happiness. We celebrated being together and feeling at one as a family. Apart from the fact that she wore pyjamas during the day, she looked like a picture of health, which made the fact that she had cancer so unreal. Who would have ever thought that we would be eating cream cakes with her and laughing the morning away? She decided to be happy and live life to the fullest that day. Never lose hope, and always think positive—that was the lesson of that day.

OCTOBER 12
MORE GOODBYES

I had to say goodbye yet again. It had become part of our routine now, and it was certainly the hardest part. We would look into each other's eyes, a little longer as time went on, and both think the same thing: *Will it be the last time?*

Then there was that last wave, starting the car and driving off, always followed by tears. At the other end of my journey, I would find the happy faces of my beautiful boys, which made me feel content and filled with love.

I had now learned from experience that if I decided on a date for my next visit to my mother, I would cope a lot better. Knowing that I had booked the return journey would give me some sort of peace of mind. It would allow me to get on with the daily routine of being a mother and not to feel guilty about not being there with her all the time. I would call her every day, and we would have little chats like we had always had, usually just about sweet little nothings. I remember on a few occasions when I would just burst into tears while on the phone. She found this hard, but she would always come out with something positive, like "But I'm still very much alive and getting better every day" and "I believe in miracles." She tried to make me live in the present rather than in the future. When I got upset, I was overcome with fear and realisation that a life without her was only just around the corner. She would tell me that nothing is over until it's over, and until that moment came, she was not dying but living.

During one of our telephone conversations, I was reading an article to her called "Walking the Way of Life" written by Ann Napier, the editor and founder of *Cygnus Community Review* (issue 7, 2011). When Ann wrote the article, she was also on a personal journey with cancer and initially uninspired to write to her readers because she says, "Who would be interested in my dark and difficult lessons that I am facing at the moment?" She even thought that perhaps she wasn't meant to write for her readers anymore. But then she slept on it and realised that she had to change her "thought form" about cancer, not to dwell on its negativity, because Ann says that this is exactly what the cancer wants. It gets fed by darkness, fear, and dread. Instead, she advices that the only way to free yourself from it is to starve it! She advises that you should nourish yourself in every way you can think of. Ann writes, "Eat and nourish yourself, even if you don't feel like it or even believe that you can; move and exercise even when pain and weakness appear to be insurmountable; appreciate and connect with others, even when that is the last thing you feel like doing." She advices giving the cancer the exact opposite of what it desires.

While I was reading this article to my mother over the phone, I could sense a shift in her energy. She had listened and had taken in the article. I felt it was making her embrace the light even more. She started looking for beauty and nourishment.

It was around this time that she started making a new sculpture, a pink angel. It was a simple and delicate piece of art, an acceptance of what was to come by making the angel but, done in a creative way, embracing the light and not the darkness. Creativity was her way of expressing emotion, and the fact that she chose to make an angel said a lot. She also went back to Tai Chi and choir practice and managed to pick up life almost as it was before. The nurses were there still twenty-four hours a day, taking care of washing my mother, doing house duties, and making coffee for visitors. It gave the whole family, including my mother, some breathing space to live a relatively "normal" life. Normal felt pretty damned good. Difficult times like we were going through make you appreciate what we do have and that the simplest things in life really are the best.

Who would have thought two months ago that my mother would be able to go for the walks again? Who would have thought that she would be driving into town to do her shopping? Who would have thought that she would be taking nature photographs to put in her diary? Who would have thought a miracle would occur after she was given only weeks to live?

The one advantage of this process is that we experience an intensely loving time together. We are aware of the dark cloud that hangs over us but enjoy the extra light that is present in the fullest, which makes us realise that every cloud has a silver lining. And as it happens, we did have a lot of sun in the last few months. I have been able to sit outside, and the warm sun on my face has given me extra strength and joy. Dianne reread my blog to me today from day one, and I really can't remember being in intensive care the first few days after surgery. I don't remember suffering in there, and it's shocking to hear that I almost didn't pull through. I'm so grateful that I did because I am having such a special and beautiful time right now. This will make it so much easier to accept that I will have to die when my time comes.

Toos

Hello, dear people,

I take very little medication at the moment, which is all relative as I have never taken any medication in my entire lifetime up to now. I am so pleased that I am getting by with just paracetamols right now. Long may it continue. Things are going reasonably well, but I do need to rest. I feel that this is of immense importance. I don't enjoy food, and I eat what's necessary. The colostomy bag still causes occasional problems, and I trust that we will find a reliable system that suits me and my situation. Just like I do every year, I enjoy the beautiful autumn. I never get bored. I keep myself busy just like the birds I watch outside. Walking in the beautiful countryside gives me positive energy. The sense of wonder and delight in the world around me has intensified since I have been ill.

Lots of sweet greetings.

Toos

Weblog: Sunday, November 13
Nine Weeks after the Diagnosis

Dear all,

I found it difficult to have a nap today because I was worried it might be the last beautiful day of autumn I will ever experience. Perhaps the last one I was ever going to be able to enjoy. The Japanese nut tree (Ginkga) has a striking yellow colour. The different types of mushrooms, which grow in the village green, are also remarkable. Yesterday was also a good day for me as I was able to go for a walk and enjoyed the outdoors. I feel pretty well at the moment and have spent some time making wreaths with crabapples from the garden. I am getting rather slim and will have to buy some new clothes. I wish you all the best.

Toos

Weblog: November 21
Normal is good

It was five years ago last week that my husband, Toon, died of cancer. After he had been diagnosed in late September, he went through a very painful but also very meaningful process. It all went downhill pretty fast, and you saw him physically decline a little every day. When I was diagnosed, it was also around the same time in September, and we as a family were expecting a similar process. On the contrary, my cancer journey is so different. I actually have hardly any pain or discomfort except the usual little aches and pains I have had for years. I seem to be getting a little better every day at the moment. I enjoy painting and am making some clay hearts. In the afternoon, I often walk in the woods (usually without the wheelchair) and have a cup of coffee somewhere nice. Sometimes I pop into the shops in the nearest little town. Yesterday I visited my niece's art exhibition. "Normal life is good."

Nobody knows how my process will develop. For now, I am choosing to enjoy my time.

Toos

It's been two and a half months already since my surgery, and I would like to share with you from the heart how I have experienced my illness so far.

I am currently feeling well. However, soon after surgery, when I had been so close to death, I experienced strong and unknown emotions. This period in the hospital was extremely difficult, due to many different factors such as pain, the morphine, the bad news, and the fact that your life is almost being lived for you with all the tests and medical interferences. However, I never felt alone during this period.

There was visible and invisible help for me. Mixed feelings of the mental and physical type passed through, some conscious and some unconscious (perhaps due to the morphine). I had to read through my own blog, which my children started for me to keep family and friends up to date, to find out what actually happened. I was probably less shocked when I read it than many of you were because in such a critical phase, a lot happens in your subconscious.

All I wished for was to be able to have time to walk through my garden, enjoy my house, and apparently, soon after the operation, I said, "Perhaps a miracle will happen." The miracle has been accomplished. I am walking in my house and garden. It's been a great gift to me, and as long as I can do that, I will want to stay alive. Meditating every day helps me stay balanced and feeds me spiritually and physically. The doctor advises to continue doing this. I meet many people with a surprised look on their faces because they heard I didn't have long to live, and they often do a double-take when they see me. I am so grateful for all you caring friends and nurses who spoil me. You give me strength to enjoy myself and to stay alive. I am still learning so much and hope my story will inspire you to make the most of your lives. I experience this "given time" as valuable time. A gift. I wouldn't have wanted to miss this phase of my life. The love and attention I am receiving is immense. The love of my family offers me comfort and wipes away my tears. I'm allowing the feeling of love and the immense power it has. The nurses are also something to be grateful for. When the moment of parting comes, it won't be easy, especially the farewell to my children and family. But we are together growing towards this moment, and I'm confident and trust that all will be well. I have finished the angel sculpture, and the angels will come and tell me when it's time to go. For now, I enjoy all things until it is time "to go home," as described in the book The Fairy Tale of Death by Marie Claire van der Bruggen.

Love from Toos

It was a gift to us, her children, that my mother was able to embrace her situation and see her time of "knowing her destiny" as a gift. Time was given to her to intensely enjoy what she had left in this lifetime with her beloved children.

Whenever anybody she knew was ill or in trouble, my mum would be there with a bunch of flowers or even a handmade sculpture crafted with her hands. She had healing hands that she would lay on people in need. In this final phase of her life, she had to learn to receive. She wrote, "I am so grateful for all the caring people; they give me strength to enjoy myself and stay alive." All this love and attention was feeding her to stay strong and positive. Wow, she was amazing, and it was like a real awakening for her and her children to appreciate the quality rather than the quantity of life.

DECEMBER 2012
MORE ROUTINE AND NORMALITY

Apart from the nurses still giving Mum full-time care, life in our family was starting to feel more normal as time went on. The nurses were becoming a bit of a dilemma because Mum was craving independence now that she was feeling so much better. She felt a real urge in her existence for things to be back as they were. She wanted to buy her own food, do her own cooking, and serve coffee to visiting family and friends. The nurses were wonderful. Some had become close friends over the months. The problem was, though, that now my mother was able to look after herself and was in need of independence. She needed to be able to reflect on what had happened to her in her own time and space. She made the decision to reduce the nursing care to evening and nighttime, when they were of most value to her at this stage of her illness. The nights were lonely and sometimes scary. It was during those dark times when the nurses were worth their weight in gold. Although my mother had faith, she must also have had her doubts at times, too. Knowing that you are going to end up in a coffin sooner rather than later must bring with it fear and anxiety. The nurses would comfort her during these emotional times in the darkness of the night, when she would open up about her true inner feelings. Often they ended up meditating together in the night. It gave the family a real sense of peace to know that somebody was with her during those times.

I was pleased that she had chosen to be alone during the day. It enabled her to fully explore her most important relationship, which was with her true self. It was, after all, her and her true self only that would have to make the transition from life to death. It was of great importance that she felt mentally comfortable in her own skin. It would certainly help the process of dying.

While I was visiting, my mum and I would occupy ourselves in a desultory but pleasant manner, doing a number of small tasks that would usually include some type of crafting. It was a passion we have always shared. It's our way of relaxing and losing ourselves in the moment. We were fully engaged in those moments and aware of how good it felt to have the gift of life.

I realised that my mother enjoyed being able to do daily tasks again, but this also made the realisation that her recovery was only temporary more testing. There was more of a contrast between the cancer and normality. She was fighting the "invisible killer," but only on the surface. She knew damn well that the cancer was terminal. The wonderful fact that she was feeling so much better had created a sadness that it was a false reality. In contrast, there was still a great deal of hope in her life. There was no hope for a miracle, though, but I wonder if that hope ever goes away. There was hope for no pain and hope for the illness to keep to a minimal state of disruption. There was also hope and desire for more gifted time. There was no pain and very little medication, and therefore her urge for living was greater. Feeling healthy and well makes you want to be alive.

I feel that I am in a new phase of my illness. This phase has good and bad sides. It's very nice that I can walk and drive again and that I am less dependent on other people. We are to reduce the nursing services, and this means that I must think and do for myself again. I reflect about what happened in the past three months and am thinking of the future and how this process will develop further. This is not always easy, and sometimes it's emotional. The days are dark in winter, and I must again get used to being alone. There is much support from my family and friends, but the realisation is that this process only concerns me with all the uncertainties that this entails. Despite all this, I still enjoy nature and going for walks. I feel that this is good for me. In nature, I can process my emotions, for which I'm grateful.

Toos

This post was written on the day that we returned to England. Me visiting and being there for her was always a welcoming distraction, but it meant that when I left, she would feel alone. Writing this now makes me realise how lonely the disease called terminal cancer must make you feel. The anguished hearts of the cancer-struck. How difficult it must be to keep your spirits high and how important love and distraction are for anybody with a terminal illness. But as my mother said, it was her journey and hers alone and one she had to walk by herself. All we could do was hold her hand to make that journey a gentler, more meaningful experience. She had to fight the demons of darkness and embrace the light, which she tried so hard to do.

She told me she was going to make her final sculpture, Archangel Michael. He would shield her from the darkness. She had been practising daily meditation for at least fifteen years prior to her illness, and Archangel Michael had been there, guiding her during meditation.

He was a symbolic figure, and making this sculpture would feed her with focus, love, light, and hope.

Weblog: December 11
Christmas greeting

I wish all friends and family a loving Christmas and hope that our hearts remain connected in 2012.

Love loves people,
believes in people, and
hopes for people.

Much love to you all,

Toos

We decided to stay home for Christmas as we do every year. The children like celebrating in their own house and so do I. The rest of the family would be there for my mother at this important family time and there would be plenty of distraction for her. She had never enjoyed this festive period much and I don't have particularly good memories of this time of year from my childhood. I believe many people struggle during the Christmas period. I decided to plan my visit on January 15 when there would be less distraction and when it would be welcome relief from the loneliness of those winter days.

December 25
Christmas Thought

Today is Christmas Day. I attended a church service this morning, and was able to sing along with my usual choir of which I am a very keen member.

I was emotional but grateful this morning that I am still alive. I feel well and enjoy everything. Your love and attention really touches me. I feel so very supported. I am grateful for the relationship that I have with my children and grandchildren.

They give me unconditional love. This love is vital to my life.

Last Monday I saw the surgeon at the hospital. His forecast in September, "a few weeks to a month." He could not believe that I walked into the room. He was also surprised at how well I looked. He spoke of a miracle! I also believe in the help of the angels. Some have wings, others live right here on earth. I find angels among my friends, family, nurses and neighbours.
Without their help, I would not have been here.
Nursing is now only at nighttime, and I am hoping that we can reduce this, as the days will get longer and brighter. I have the feeling that I have some more time to enjoy here on earth. Who knows, I may reach ninety!
I wish you, on behalf of myself and all my children, a peaceful Christmas and happy holidays. And always keep faith, like me, for miracles in your life.

Toos

How glad I am that she was grateful and enjoyed being here with us, her loved ones, on that particular Christmas Day. The subject wasn't discussed, but we all knew that it was most probably her last Christmas ever, and by reading her post, I think she knew that, too. This thought must have been difficult for her. I wonder what went through her mind when she bravely put up her Christmas decorations. I find that putting up and taking down decorations confronts me with the passing of time. Where has the year gone? My hat off to her for sticking to the traditions, where we can often be met by negative thoughts.

I rang her first thing that Christmas morning to wish her a happy day. She appreciated the early call and was looking forward to going singing with her church choir. We resisted talking about anything too heavy. I was just relieved she was OK, and it made me able to enjoy my day at home with my little family without any feelings of guilt. I was grateful to my sister, who spent Christmas with her. She told me that they kept the day quiet with meditation. They went to a place of silence, where they were able to have philosophical reflection and meet the God within us all. This was followed by a peaceful dinner with my brother, Peter, and his wife Marian. The joy for my family came from keeping it simple, without having any commitments or high expectations.

Weblog: January 16, 2012
Four and a Half Months after the Diagnosis
Time of Rest

I can probably speak for everybody when I say, "Glad it's January."
The countdown to the end of the year was particularly emotional
because I felt confronted and anxious about the New Year lurking
around the corner, which is most probably the year I'll die.

Christmas periods at the best of times are busy. Perhaps that's why I
am extra tired at the moment. I certainly need my afternoon naps.

I have also been making a sculpture for a retiring priest who has been
an inspiration to me over the years. He retired on January 11, hence
the pressure of having to finish it. The "having to" was also tiring, but
I am pleased I pushed myself and am happy with the end result.

I find it important and nice to occasionally be alone, to meditate and
to reach a deeper connection to my inner self. I feel that I get help
from all angles.

There is so much love around me. I would like to give you each a heart.

As you can see in this picture, I try, for as long as I can, to realise this wish.

I feel positive and happy this week because my daughter Dianne and my youngest grandchild, Rufus, are coming over from England for a few days. Rufus and I have a lot of fun together. He is as pure as can be, with not a care in the world.

Love, Toos

JANUARY 15–17, 2012

The long journey was as always a good transition period between my two homes. The one I made in England and the one I left in Holland. My feelings were happy to be released during these journeys and I would not fight them either. Two-year-old Rufus would question my tears and I would happily explain to him why I was sad as we talked about his grandmother's illness on his level. I would tell him that she was very poorly and that it makes me sad because I don't like to see her poorly. I left the death bit until later in the process as I didn't feel it necessary for him to worry about that. Better I think that I just lived in the moment with him and that I answered his questions as best I could.

During this particular visit we decided to stay at my brother's house next door to my mother's so we could come and go depending on my mother's need for rest.

Since her operation, she still appeared to be recovering, and on the outside, at least, she looked pretty amazing. We all knew very well, however, that the cancer was eating her on the inside. During my father's cancer, which lasted only about two and a half months from diagnosis, he looked more ill every time I visited. The cancer was visibly eating him away, with a lot of pain to deal with. But in my mother's case, the process was very different. It was enjoyable to go home without too many dark thoughts attached. It was a time for enjoying each other to the fullest extent while we still had time to do so. There was no immediate danger in her health, and we would live in the moment and enjoy each other's company and love.

The moment of our arrival was one of pure joy, and we found her sitting in her chair with a big smile on her face, arms open, ready for a hug and a kiss. During her illness, she found her real wealth in the simple things. Just being with her family, sitting silently and enjoying their presence would give her most delight. She also enjoyed the scent of flowers and the sound of the birds more intensely than she ever did before. Everybody who dies has to leave their monetary wealth, but in their hearts they can take the spiritual and emotional wealth of the heart, the love that enriched their lives, and the love that can never die. Real wealth is being able to experience and accept the simple things in life as a gift: a smile, a wink, a flower, or the sound of a bird singing.

Our arrival that day was one of those simple gifts, but it was also something for her to look forward to and focus on for the proceeding days. The beginning of our stay, the reuniting, was, as always, the best part. She would be looking forward to our reunion, and it was a real welcoming distraction from her illness. A moment of total joy and love, a time of forgetting everything else going on but just a moment of living in the present. She always chose to make this particular "meeting again moment" a happy one.

Once we had settled down after the initial excitement of seeing each other again, I realised that it was nice not to have the nurses there during the day. It felt more like how it used to be before she was ill. My mother and I had a very easy and uncomplicated relationship, so it was always quite blissful to be with her. We didn't need to talk and just enjoyed being one as a mother and daughter. We used to potter around a lot, something that made us both happy.

She told me that she had decided that she wanted to buy my sister and me a beautiful ring each, and we would choose them in the jewellery shop together. My mother was one of ten children and didn't have much jewellery that she had inherited or bought in her lifetime. So she wanted to give her daughters a nice ring in her memory. We drove to my sister's house, and had lunch with her. Everything that day appeared like it used to be, and again I felt intensely happy and grateful to have this unexpected normality with her again, five months after her operation. Who would have thought I would be having lunch and laughter with my mother and sister, followed by a trip to the shops?

We drove to the jewellery shop together, and the lady in the shop showed us many different boxes filled with precious stones and rings. We were able to design our own unique piece by choosing different elements that would then be compiled into a ring. All our eyes fell on a beautiful green jewel, the colour of my eyes. We chose this beautiful precious stone called Prehnite to be the centerpiece of the ring. We designed the ring around this stone that we felt was the one for me. During the hour or so that we were in the shop, again I felt intensely blessed to have my mother and sister there by my side. I knew it was probably the last time we would be out shopping together. Rather than letting that thought upset me, I let myself enjoy the time even more. I wear this gift of a ring with so much love attached to it. It's no wonder that Prehnite symbolises unconditional love.

I was aware that my visit to Holland was quickly coming to an end. At least I could leave with a happy feeling, knowing Mum had settled back in at home well and that she was content there for the time being. Living at home on her own was improving her well-being, and it gave her time to reflect about what she had gone through over the previous five months. Although she did get tired quickly and needed to rest on a regular basis, she was managing pretty well on her own, having the nurses with her through the nighttime. I found this short poem, "Aubade" by Philip Larkin, that attempts to explain the fear that cancer may cause at night. It helps me understand why she wanted somebody to be near during the nights.

No sight, no sound
No touch or taste or smell, nothing to think with
Nothing to love or link with,
The anaesthetic from which none come 'round.

JANUARY 18
FOUR AND A HALF MONTHS AFTER THE DIAGNOSIS

Yet another morning had come around when I had to say goodbye before I made my way back to England. Again, we had the longer-than-usual eye contact with that same thought running through our minds: *Will this be the last time we ever see each other?* In the previous four months, I have had more intense eye contact with my mother than I have probably had since I was feeding from her breasts. This time, though, I felt pretty certain it wasn't going to be the last time our eyes would meet.

I was happy to drive home after a lovely visit and to go back to what seemed an uncomplicated little life in England. On the one hand, being a long way away made things a lot more difficult because I couldn't visit her at my own leisure. On the other hand, my life in England hadn't been affected on a day-to-day level. We spoke to each other every day on the phone. She sounded the same through the phone as she always had. My mother appeared well, and while she was happy getting on with her life in Holland, living in the moment, I was happily doing the same in England. Her next goal in life was to comfortably get to her birthday on January 31. There wasn't a doubt in my mind that she would reach her seventy-sixth birthday.

Weblog: January 25
Another Birthday Coming...

It's hard to believe that the first month of 2012 is already coming to an end. On January 31 I am hoping to celebrate my seventy-sixth birthday! My seventy-fifth birthday was celebrated exuberantly with family, friends, and acquaintances while I was blissfully unaware that it would be my last big party.

This year, I celebrate my birthday in peace with just the children and grandchildren at Peter and Marian's house. Given my health situation, I can't cope with much more. Too many visitors and people talking at once make me really, really tired. What feeds me most are my walks, taking rest, and making time for reflection and meditation.

Love, Toos

I decided not to go to Holland to celebrate her birthday with her. It wasn't something that I usually did anyway. Once, during my twenty-five years of living in England, I surprised her on her birthday by making an unexpected visit. I remember it being a busy day full of talking sweet nothings with aunties, uncles, and friends. Instead, I decided to visit for a week with the boys. We booked a holiday cottage during half-term in the middle of February. I felt that this would result in a higher-quality visit. When her birthday arrived, I didn't have any sense of guilt that I wasn't there to celebrate in person. I made sure, as always, that I spoke to her first on her special day by making an early-morning call before any of my brothers and sister had arrived in person to congratulate her. We didn't treat this birthday any differently than all the others. We just chatted about this and that and about her plans for the day. We were protecting each other from the "other" reality.

Weblog: February 6
Life "Just" Goes On...

Despite predictions and beyond expectations, my life has got into a "normal" routine again. Many friends came to say their farewells in the early weeks of my illness and are now coming back for second or third times. It seems very clear that nobody knows what awaits us tomorrow. In my case, "tomorrow" was above expectations. The days roll into weeks and even months. I am currently not feeling ill, and actually things are going well. I am often tired, though, and need my afternoon nap.

My birthday was quiet and pleasant with the children and grandchildren. I even made a wonderful new discovery: Chinese food! I find it really tasty, and it's wonderful to be able to enjoy food again, which I hadn't been able to for quite a while. I enjoy my walks and have been gathering natural little treasures in the forests. I have taken many photographs of the natural beauty I am finding around me. I turn these photos into cards to send to family and friends. It's so important for me to have little projects like these to give me a focus in life. Thanks for all your lovely cards, flowers, and messages on the blog. I was particularly spoiled on my birthday. Toos

FEBRUARY
FIVE MONTHS AFTER THE DIAGNOSIS

The holiday cottage was just a few miles up the road from my mother's house. There was a swimming pool in the park where I would leave the older two boys for some fun swimming while Rufus and I would make brief visits to my mother.

We wanted to make the most of our time together. Ever since her birthday in January, she had started to feel more tired and was visibly losing weight more quickly. It was a clear sign that we were now moving closer and faster towards the inevitable.

She was, however, still able to drive and would visit us in our holiday home. We went for refreshing walks through the park, where we would sit on a bench while watching the boys have fun in the playground. Seeing Rufus's happy face as he slid down the slide would put a beaming smile onto her face. The older two boys, who were aware of the situation, did their best to make the most of their time with Oma. We were yet again blessed with real quality time. On the outside, she looked well, but on the inside the cancer was now clearly eating her away.

We talked about sweet little nothings a lot and wanted to just be normal and happy while we could. In the evening, my sister and her children and my mother came for dinner in our holiday home. She didn't eat much, but it felt special to be together.

Weblog: February 17
Nobody Knows

I am writing this message in a cozy holiday cottage, where Dianne and her children are staying. My daughters (Dianne and Ans), their children, and I are enjoying each other's company while we philosophise about the further course of the disease. We made the conclusion that "Nobody knows."

I feel that my body is getting more and more tired. The flip side of this is that I am sleeping very well. Food is something I really don't enjoy these days, and I am therefore continually losing more and more weight. I feel grateful to still be taking my daily walk. When you don't see me going for these walks anymore, you will know that things aren't well.

I don't have much to write about at the moment, as times are quiet with very little news. My life now is not so much about doing but more about being.

Much love to you all.

Toos x

When it was time for my mum to leave our holiday cottage, she asked me to walk to the car with her, where a few boxes of goodies were awaiting me. It had become a tradition that whenever we came to Holland, she would buy us a box of goodies from the health shop mixed in with some luxury gifts of facial creams and bath oils for me. It turned out to be the last box of goodies ever. I knew deep down and she probably did too.

The dreaded day of leaving came along all too soon. This time the parting was more intense than our parting on the previous few visits. The realisation that our time together was nearing felt stronger than in the months before. She was starting to lose control of her life.

Weblog: March 11
Slowly

Since celebrating my birthday on January 31, I feel that things are slowly taking a turn and that my health is declining. I need more rest, eat less, and pain is taking its toll. Last Thursday, there was no other choice than going back to the morphine plasters. Thankfully, the dose is still relatively low. I had an incident on Wednesday while having a walk through the village. It was a rainy day, and I was carrying an umbrella. When a lorry passed, the umbrella caught the wind, which resulted in a fall. I am still suffering pain as a result of it.

The good news is that spring is coming. The birds are building their nests while singing beautifully, and the crocuses and tulips are popping their little heads up toward the light. New life is coming. I'm longing for it to get warmer soon so I can enjoy the spring sunshine and warmth from my garden chair. I enjoyed some sunshine today, which was a positive experience. Pleased to tell you that my hands are still busy making sculptures, though, be it slowly and in very small steps. I have started a new sculpture of Archangel Michael with whom I've had a strong connection for a long time. This angel gives me love, power and light. He sadly broke a wing this week, but I will repair that. I would like to make more hearts too as these are less physical work. I want so much still in my mind, but my body doesn't want to play.

I am sending you my love and will be back.

Toos x

Weblog: March 27
Enjoying Time in the Garden

Once again, I feel that I am drifting into a new phase in which I need to rest even more. Precious time is moving along while my life energy levels are dropping. In addition to taking small doses of morphine, I have to listen to my body and take it very slowly to enable times of enjoyment. My body has been feeling very unbalanced since the fall. I have to keep warm, which luckily hasn't been too much of an effort during those beautiful sunny days we've had lately. I have enjoyed watching my sisters and sons while they worked in my garden, getting it ready for spring. It looks beautiful. My son, Peter, and his wife, Marian, share their evening meal with me on a daily basis. I feel blessed with the love and support I feel all around me. Both emotional and practical support make such an amazing difference to the quality of my life.

Love from Toos

EASTER
SIX AND A HALF MONTHS AFTER THE DIAGNOSIS
The boys had two weeks off for their Easter break. If only we had our own little place over in Holland so that we could be around my mum and pop in every day to be with her. For us to stay at her house is something of the past now. She needed quiet. A family with three boys

certainly wouldn't bring her that. My brothers and sister had all invited us to stay, but again I didn't want to invade their houses with a family of young boys.

I felt pulled about where to go this particular Easter break because I also wanted to be there for one of my best friends, who was going through a very difficult divorce. I had promised her months earlier that we would go see them. It highlighted the fact that it's difficult to plan ahead when you have a loved one who is terminally ill.

Unfortunately, my friend and my mum were in totally different directions from where we live. They were five hours away—one to the east and one to the west. What I really wanted was to just stay put, chill out, and enjoy our Easter break at home with not a worry in the world. Sadly, there wasn't anywhere near that state of contentment, and I felt bad letting this thought even cross my mind while my mum was dying and one of my friends was going through a lonely divorce. We decided to split the holidays in two and see both my friend and my mother.

The boys were happy to see their Oma. After having lost their aunties and granddad through sudden death only a year earlier, it must have been special for them to have this time to say goodbye to her. They seemed at peace with it. I tried to talk to them about her dying but found it hard to get through to them. They were reluctant to talk about their grandmother's illness and the emotions that went with it. Probably in their eyes, six months on from when she was in intensive care, they were seeing her again, looking thin, but happy and beautiful. This must have made them feel that life doesn't always get torn away fast like it had been in their auntie's and grandfather's case. I hope this was comforting to them.

When their aunties died so suddenly, it was incomprehensible and dark. How could a child understand? One day they came over for coffee, and the next day they had died. During this dark time, just like this time in my mother's case, they wouldn't discuss what had happened and avoided anything being said about the subject. Some good books are available to help children communicate when grieving, including my own one, *Remembering*. They help children work through their grief in a creative way, through drawing and writing down their feelings about the person who died at their own pace. My children must have been affected in a way similar to the way I was as a young child, being confronted with the vulnerability of life at such a young age and realising so early on that nobody knows what's around the corner.

With my mum, they were told six months earlier that she would die within weeks. But at least this time, they were able to go see her and say farewell, not expecting to visit her again six months later. Somehow I think this must have given them hope and more security for the future. Loved ones don't always get torn out of our lives in an instant. The boys learned that sometimes there is time to say goodbye and together we lived toward the moment when this time of dying would finally come. We were all preparing, in our own private ways, to let her go.

The weeks over Easter were memorable. I was able to spend precious time with my mother on my own, while my husband looked after the children. While being with her one on one, it soon became apparent that the pain was getting her down. From experience with my dad, she knew damn well that worse was still to come. She told me that if she had to suffer increasing pain, life wouldn't be worth living. Consequently she started talking about what she wanted at the funeral. It was hard to discuss this with her, but she was adamant that I knew what her few wishes were. Really, there was only one thing that was obviously important to her: she wanted the church to be decorated with pink flowers everywhere. Apart from that, she told me that everything would be well cared for by her children.

We talked about her death and the illness for some of the time, but nothing gave us more pleasure than just being together, talking about sweet nothings, something we had always been so good at. I think while she was ill that we spent 10 percent of the time talking about death, illness, and feelings, and the rest was kept to light, normal, day-to-day chitchat just like anybody, with or without a terminal illness, would do. I believe it was probably the same with her friends who came to visit.

Probably one in ten would talk more in-depth about her situation, and the rest would act normally, just visiting like they did when she was healthy and well. There was one big difference, though, compared to visits when she was well. Every visitor who left after spending time with her had the same thought: *Will this be the last time I see her?* How do you say goodbye to somebody who is likely to die soon? Personally, I think "See you soon" is appropriate, actually. Anybody, in theory, could die tomorrow! I can only imagine how exhausting it must be for somebody with terminal illness to go through an emotional goodbye every time he or she parts with a family member or friend.

I have to admit, though, that while staying in Holland with her for a few days, it was a lot easier to say goodbye every evening and pop over to my brother's next door for the night than it was when I was going back home to England.

Weblog: April 10
Archangel Michael

I have managed to finish the sculpture of Archangel Michael with just a little help from a fellow artist friend. I could have made some more adjustments to make it better, but I am content about leaving it the way it is now. Archangel Michael is fighting the dragon, and he wins. He is the most powerful, celebrated, and well-known angel in history, scripture, art, and literature. He stands for light, protection, deliverance, and faith. Archangel Michael uses a warrior's strength to protect us from the sons of darkness.

I believe that this will be the last-ever sculpture I will produce. A friend gave me a candle with Archangel Michael on it that I will light when there is an ever-greater need for his healing powers. I feel that I am getting weaker, have more pain, and need to sleep more. It is easy to accept that the medication is increasing. I am hoping that this will improve the quality of my life. I would like to go for walks again, even if it's just a short one around the village green. Dianne and her family are over from England, and I thoroughly enjoy seeing my grandchildren. Thank you to everybody for all the attention and kind words in your loving cards. They really do make a difference.

Toos

The next day, we took some pictures for her weblog of her with her new sculpture, *Archangel Michael*. We loved just pottering together, finding a good spot to take the picture, and writing some words for the weblog. Actually, writing down the posts for her weblog was extremely therapeutic because it forced us to feel and think about what was really going on in her life and in our lives. We would talk together about her illness and about the feelings that went with it. In this particular post, she said that this would be the last sculpture she would make in her life and that after our little photo session, she realised she hadn't signed the sculpture. She just did it without giving it much thought, but for me, this was a really emotional moment. I stood behind her, watching her sign her last signature. It was a sobering reality check for me. This was really a final moment, something my mother would never do again, but then she would never cycle or drive the car again, either. But to actually witness something that was final was tough for me. I realise now that she was probably pleased to finalise her angel, Michael, because he gave her so much comfort. She used to tell me that if she felt scared or tearful, she would call on Archangel Michael and that she would feel his energy, which would make her feel warm all over. This angel was ready now to guide her through to the next phase, to be there when she would pass on.

Just a few months earlier, I had stepped into my mother's footsteps and embarked on a course of pottery and ceramics, which was one of my lifetime wishes. She enjoyed seeing what I made, and after signing her final sculpture, she was thrilled to pass all her tools on to me, from mother to daughter. Somehow, I started to realise that the circle of her life was completing. We talked through the different tools and their various uses, and it was another momentous moment when she gave me her basket full of artistic equipment. To this day, I use the tools with great care and try to create with love, just like my mother did.

After only an hour or so, she was getting visibly tired. My mum was no longer the woman with buckets full of energy she used to be. That was a reality that she and I had to deal with. My time had come to look after her now. Although she was still an enormous support to me in an emotional way, we couldn't do some of the more physical things that we enjoyed before. She couldn't cook us dinner anymore or make my boys their well-loved "Oma picnic" full of delicacies and surprises to take on the long trip home. All these losses were easy to accept, though, while she was still here with us having reasonable quality of life with moments of intense joy and love.

The next day, my sister joined us in the afternoon. It always felt complete when the three of us spent time together as mother and daughters. No complexity was left in our relationships. During the months of her illness, any issues became insignificant, and the love we felt for each was more intense and beautiful than ever. I have three sons, and I believe a son-mother relationship is often a straight-forward one, but daughter-mother bonds tend to be a little more complex. The advantage of having time during my mother's illness to communicate deeply is that any issues concerning these relationships could be solved. I advise anybody reading this book that if there are things bothering you in your relationship with a parent, please do discuss it. Often these "set in stone" family patterns can be solved if you take the first step to talk about them. It's a difficult thing to do, but it's necessary to move on. I believe that often the parent is not aware of the problem and would do anything to help. It could be a small thing that was said when you were small that has affected you all your life.

Because all of our issues were addressed and solved, my mother, my sister, and I were free to think about what we wanted to talk about, things we might regret not having asked once she had died. We decided to talk about our individual births—how she experienced our births and what happened in detail. It turned out that I was born during the most terrible rainstorm and my father wasn't present because he got stuck in the mud when he was picking up the midwife in the middle of the night. It was fascinating stuff.

One of my brothers joined us a bit later, and it felt special to be together. It made me realise that I was blessed to have been born into such a warm nest. We all realised that this time was precious. It was something that didn't need to be said, but it was something we were all thinking. We felt intense happiness being together, but the flip side of that was realisation of the imminent end to that time together, in the warmth of my mother in my mother's house.

The next day came, and my week in Holland was over already. As in the previous months, the most difficult part of visiting was saying goodby every time I left for England, I couldn't help thinking, *Will this be the last time?*

On that particular day, Mum chose not to come outside to wave us out, a ritual that had become a tradition with us hooting our horns and waving with big smiles on our faces until she was completely out of sight. Instead, she stood behind the window, waving. She looked thin and frail. Another freeze frame was created in my memory that I won't forget. This time, the eye contact while we shared looking through the window had so much sadness attached to it. The previous few months, I had felt pretty confident that I would see her again. But this time, with the glass between us, it felt different, as if she was slowly moving further away. We were both being strong for each other, but I noticed her eyes well up. The darkness was slowly creeping in. I felt that the farewell to my beloved mother was getting close. I didn't stay in the moment for too long and got into the car quite swiftly. I was keeping strong for the boys and my mum, but of course it didn't take long before the music would provoke my tears.

I was so glad to have my own little family. They kept me going and pulled me through. I was talking about this to a friend who has no children. I was telling her how much harder it would have been with no children. I am so happy that she put me in my place by telling me happiness shouldn't come from your children but from within. Thank you!

Weblog: April 28
Dutch Queen's Day

It's Queen's Day, a happy and festive day in our country. I have always felt a connection with our queen because we were both born on the January 31, me being slightly older by just two years. Due to my illness, I won't be able to experience the festivities in the village and around the country. I have therefore decided to really spoil myself. I am going to make my own experience of how it feels to be queen for the day. My daughter, Ans, took me out to buy a beautiful dress, we bought flowers in the national colours of the land, and my son, Peter, has made the cross for Archangel Michael, who is now complete. Peter took the perfect picture of me being queen.

Apart from the excitement of posing as the queen, things are quiet and slow. The pain is bearable, I have less energy every day, and I'm not walking much anymore—just a few minutes around the garden at times. In the house, I use a walker, and hopefully this will benefit me for some more time to come. But a friend told me yesterday, "You are not going backward, but forward toward the angels." I liked that thought.

Mum was going through a new phase of growth, moving on and arriving into the winter of her life, more radiant than ever as her inner light shone through. It was a beauty that came from the very core of her being, which can be achieved after many years of life experience.

MAY
EIGHT MONTHS AFTER THE DIAGNOSIS

The plan was for Rufus and me to set off very early and catch the 5:50 a.m. shuttle. I never sleep well when I have to travel early the following day, and that night was no exception. On top of the usual clock watching, Rufus was crying and sick most of the night. The alarm was set for 4:50 a.m. If I had left with a sick child with five hours of travelling following a two-hour sleep, I would have been irresponsible. I decided at four o'clock to cancel the alarm and see what would happen. Rufus woke up at his usual time of 6:50 a.m., bright as a button. In the end, I managed to set off at eight o'clock. It was so nice to have Rufus on these journeys because he always managed to lighten things up. He never failed to get excited about our long journeys to Holland to see his Oma. He knew she was ill, but that didn't take away any of the excitement of going. I thought it was unlikely that she would suddenly die, and the fact that she had cancer was something that I had come to terms with. I spoke to her every day, and her voice sounded just like it always had, but seeing her was always different than before. Even though going there had become part of the routine, it was strange and much more trying in those last few months, especially after not seeing her for weeks. I just knew she was going to look thinner and sicker.

The cancer was eating her away. For the first time in her life, she looked slim, something she had always tried to achieve. But she looked slim for the wrong reasons. One part of me thought, *Wow, she looks amazing as a slim woman, and I could look really good if I did some work on myself.* On the other hand, I felt sad that she was slim because she couldn't enjoy food anymore. We had both always found food one of the biggest pleasures in life, and that joy was torn away from her now. She was eating to live, not the other way around!

When we finally arrived, there was, as always, a radiant smile on her face. She loved seeing Rufus, who she often called her little angel. She believed, like me, that he was a gift from my father. She would cuddle him and blow him kisses. An innocent child who didn't realise that she was gravely ill—what a fantastic comfort that must have been. It makes me sad that he probably won't remember her when he grows up, but I believe he will carry the love she gave him throughout his life in his heart. I will do my very best to keep her memories alive.

Once I had opened the door to the house and made eye contact with Mum, the atmosphere was always light, with a true feeling of euphoria because we were reunited, and we knew we had a lot of time together coming up, or at least it felt that way. Two days wasn't a long time at all.

My oldest and one of my dearest friends, Emma, had lived on the green where my mother's house was with me when I was a child. She now lives in Cape Town. By pure chance, she happened to be in the village during this visit, which was the icing on the cake for me. We hadn't seen each other for seven years, even though we had shared most of our childhood and our most intimate secrets. And here she was by pure chance, a friend in need, indeed. We arranged that she would come over to see my mother the next morning.

The day before our arrival, my mother had called to tell me to bring back some of her sculpting tools because she decided that she would like to make another sculpture after all. She felt she needed to keep herself occupied to stay positive. She needed a focus and distraction. Although making a sculpture really was physically too hard for her, she had asked me to start her off by doing the heavy-duty basic work by making some sort of world, and she would than put little human figures on top of it that would symbolise all her nearest and dearest children and grandchildren. She had planned this for the next few days, so there would be plenty to keep us occupied.

But the day of our arrival, we just enjoyed being together. The doctor came, and we talked about the roller-coaster ride she was on. How amasing it was that she kept bouncing back after difficult weeks. One week, I would think she would die soon, and the next, I thought she may have another year. It was a pretty scary ride with only one certainty: death! It was amazing how she had dealt with it up to that point, giving the impression she wasn't scared.

The thing that bothered her the most was how her illness would develop. We have control of a lot of things in life, but we can't control the way our lives will end, although this was not the case in Liz's death. Nearly all of us wonder when and how we die at times, but if you know you are terminally ill and that there is no hope of long-term survival, it must dwell in your thoughts on a regular basis. And, of course the answer is "Nobody knows." I tried to put myself into her shoes sometimes, imagining how it would feel to know you are so near death's door. I would hope that I would be able to see each day as a little lifetime in itself, but that I would also be able to release tears and hopefully have my loved ones there with me as much as possible to get through it. A quote I've heard says, "You can conquer everything when there is love in your life."

The next morning, when Rufus and I walked over to my mum's house (my brother's house, where we were staying, was only next door), we looked through the window where her bed was in the front lounge looking out onto the village green, to make sure she was up. Unfortunately she had already gone back to bed for a rest, and it was only 9:00 a.m. She needed so much more sleep. Looking through that window, it was sad to see her so lifeless, lying on her bed. I couldn't help wondering if that is how she would look dead. Rufus and I went back to my brother's house and returned to look through the window half an hour later. This time, she heard us, and she was visibly moved to see Rufus waving excitedly through the window at her.

After her little rest while the early-morning pain had a chance to subside, we enjoyed coffee together, and it didn't take long before my friend, Emma, arrived to join us. There was a lot of reminiscing about the old days, and it made me happy to have one of my dearest friends, who was so fond of my parents, there with us. Talking about the past was something we had in common; talking about the future was something we didn't have in common. I believe that people who are terminally ill enjoy talking about the past more because talking about the future makes them realise that they may not be there, and it can therefore make them sad. After we had coffee Emma didn't want to say goodbye to my mother yet and postponed that difficult task until the next day. She was to leave for South Africa again, so it was pretty certain that they would never see each other again after the next day. I totally understood that she wanted to slightly delay her farewell.

From 12:00 p.m. to 2:00 p.m., my mum would rest while Rufus and I would step back into normal life for a shopping trip in the local town. When we came back, my sister-in-law, Marian, looked after Rufus so my mum and I could have some time together to embark on a new venture, the sculpture. She found the colour of clay she wanted and instructed me where we would set up our little clay-making base. It was a lovely day, so she decided to sit outside. As we were working on the sculpture, things were so peaceful and normal. This could have been at any stage of our lives together, just being together and creating. Although I was doing the more physical work, she was also helping and telling me how to do it. Creativity made us forget everything, and those few hours were precious. It didn't take long to make the basics of the sculpture, and then it was time to make the little abstract people. They were only about 10 cm high and 2 cm wide, so not labour-intensive to make. She had already made two little figures while I was struggling with the first. It made me realise how talented she was at sculpting. She even managed to shape them into little characters with real personalities. We had a real giggle talking about the different characters who symbolised all the siblings in our family and the way they were interacting together. She was visibly relaxing and forgetting about everything while she focused on her creations. She taught me not to be scared with the clay and to let shapes evolve. I was inspired by the way she did this. I was pleased that she managed to think of a way that she could escape the cancer for a little while. She was tired but fulfilled afterwards.

My mother had another rest while I cooked for her and my sister-in-law, Marian. She had been cooking for my mum for the previous three months or so and would bring her dinner over from next door every evening. Mum hadn't been enjoying her food for some time and wasn't really in a fit state to cook for herself anymore, so I suggested that we cook for them tonight so we could have a family dinner in my mum's house once more. Her house had always been the place to entertain the family. But in the previous six months, she hadn't been able to do this. It was lovely for me to turn back the clock a little to how it used to be. All in all it had been a very special day and I was looking forward to spending more time with her the next day.

I think she had thoroughly enjoyed our time together because the next morning when Rufus and I looked for her through the window the bed was empty. We walked into the house where she was already sitting in her chair waiting for us to come. I made her coffee and we chatted. Emma came back to say goodbye. I left them to it and waited for her outside. She came out saying "I don't have the feeling that this was the last time." Who knows? Nobody knows when goodbyes are the last goodbyes. Always make sure goodbyes are without negative energy is what I think, and perhaps Emma saying or believing it was not the last time she would ever see her might have been a coping mechanism, and perhaps that wasn't a bad idea.

I spent that afternoon at my sister's house. We would have liked my mother to join us, but she declined, using the excuse that if she wasn't there, we could do whatever we wanted and didn't have to be held back because of her being there. It's just as well that she didn't come because Rufus threw the tantrum of all tantrums that lasted over an hour.

When I got back that evening, we sat in the garden together on her meditation bench, enjoying the sunset, the birds, and each other's company, both aware that we had to part again the next morning. The silence between us was so peaceful. The previous afternoon, we were *doing* together, and that evening we were *being* together. We had managed to create a perfect balance between the two, and the visit had been one of mainly happy emotions.

Waking up that morning, I was filled with the dread of having to say goodbye to her again. This was always the worst part of my visits, and it wouldn't be normal if my main thought wasn't *Is this the last time I will see her?* Because she seemed better than she had during my previous visit, I presumed that it wouldn't. This time, she came outside to wave us out, and of course little Rufus lightened the experience, not realising what the reality was and just living in the moment in his innocent little way. I was wondering how many more times I was emotionally capable of saying goodbye to her like this. In my head, I decided to keep it light and said, "Thanks for the lovely days, Mum. See you again soon. Take good care, and I will call you when I get home." There was again that precious moment of eye contact. In that precious little moment so much emotion was exchanged. Then, as we had done for the previous twenty-five years, we hooted and waved as she slowly disappeared out of our view. Soon after she disappeared, the tears would follow, as always. The CD of 2011 that had been stuck in my car CD player for the previous six months was "21" by Adele. It had more than a few tearjerkers among its song collection. I couldn't help but think that my mum had "set fire to the rain." She had achieved so much more than was predicted when first diagnosed. She had let the cancer in and allowed it to be there, but she was still the one controlling it with her burning desire for life that came from within.

Weblog: May 11
Something New Again. (This would be her last-ever post on the blog.)

I am finding that the best way of keeping me motivated for living is through using my hands. If I don't stay creative, my mind takes over with worries and anxieties of what is to come. I am able to express my feelings through my hands and will keep going for as long as possible. A month ago, I finished what I believed was my last-ever sculpture. Well, it wasn't! My hands "itch" when I stop, and I started a new sculpture yesterday. Dianne started it off for me. The beginning of making a sculpture can be quite labour-intensive, so thank you, Dianne, for helping me. She made a kind of round, earth-shaped base on which I will be fixing little human figures that symbolise my family. All my children, children-in-law, and grandchildren will take place on the earth. Making the little figures isn't too labour-intensive, and I can sit down while making them. They are abstract little figures, but I'm trying to put some character into each one of them. In turn, every single family member is passing through my hands where I try and shape them with all my love. I can still enjoy being in this beautiful world. I have never heard the birds sing like I have this year. I feed them, and in return they gift me their song. While enjoying the birds with my doctor last week, he told me that his mother used to tell him that when the birds sing, they pray. Perhaps that is true.

Spring greetings from Toos x

MAY-JUNE
EIGHT TO NINE MONTHS AFTER THE DIAGNOSIS
BACK IN ENGLAND

I spoke to Mum on the phone every day. She knew it was hard for me to have only phone contact. In the twenty-five years that I had lived in England, I had to miss a lot of the family's good times, but this year also very much the difficult times. My family all lived so close together, and during weekends and birthday parties, I always felt alone in England because I couldn't be part of it. So during this period in May and June, she would do her utmost to give the impression that she was doing OK. But talking about the weather and sweet nothings became harder for her. I could tell she wasn't so interested in what I had been doing, and when I asked her one day how she was feeling mentally, she totally broke down on the phone. It was almost as if she was only just coming to terms with her illness and that she was falling into depression. She told me how low and lonely she felt and that sitting in her house looking outside at the world continuing, as if nothing had happened, made her feel empty and strange. Because she had given me the impression of things going so-so and OK, I hadn't quite realised how difficult the previous few weeks, since I left, had been for her, as well as for my siblings and the in-laws.

She had been quite negative about not being able to do anything. She complained that she didn't enjoy eating, walking was too painful and difficult, and she often forgot in the afternoon who had been visiting in the morning. She found it almost impossible to put a smile on her face and seemed to have fallen into a deep depression. The doctor prescribed antidepressants, and very soon after that, she began getting very confused. She didn't know what was going on and didn't seem to remember how long she had been ill. She complained about not feeling anything anymore. It was soon decided to stop the antidepressants.

My phone calls to my mother were not the same, and I could tell that she was trying hard to make a good impression, asking questions about the children, but she wasn't engaged. I found this time extremely difficult because our phone calls had always been the only connection I had with my mother while I was at home in England. It was a connection we had made every day since my father died six years earlier.

In a strange way, the little bit of my mother I was able to have in England had already died, and I was avoiding ringing because it was too distressing for me to listen to her. I remember ringing her out of duty on Sunday, June 3, 2012, a big day in England because it was the Queen's Diamond Jubilee. I couldn't stop crying when I spoke to her because I didn't know where to turn or what to do.

I had different siblings saying different things. One said, "I think you should come soon because it isn't going well at all," and the other would say, "Oh, stay at home. She isn't in danger." On the one hand, I so craved some days at home with the kids, and on the other hand, I felt this pull toward Holland. I was so emotionally and physically exhausted from packing and unpacking. All I wanted to do was curl up and cry and have my normal life back.

I felt guilty that I was hoping it would all be over soon, that she would die soon. It was so exhausting to know for eight months that your mother's death is imminent, but nobody knows when. My life was on hold, and it couldn't get calm and balanced until my mother was dead. How awful that I had these thoughts, but I just couldn't help it. I hated leaving my children every month, and my mum had got to a stage where she couldn't really cope with my two-year-old Rufus anymore. That meant I had to go on my own.

I was on the edge of breaking down. When I spoke to Mum, I just cried on the phone, asking her for advice on what to do. Should I come or not? Who shall I bring? She said, "That's not up to me—whatever feels right for you." The problem was that I didn't know what felt right for me anymore. She told me she would like me to come with the whole family and she would pay for a holiday cottage for us to stay in. My brother Toon then asked to speak to me and told me not to give my mum emotional pressure like this because she couldn't cope with it anymore. That disturbed me even more because I felt that this phone communication was the only bit of my mother I had left while at home in England. I felt that my brother was being insensitive towards my situation, but of course he was only protecting my mother and doing what was right for her. I couldn't really judge how it would be to be there with her anymore. Her personality had changed and our roles were now really starting to reverse. I was scared about how I would find her.

In the end, we decided that we would go with the whole family for a long weekend. The fact that we had made up our minds about this gave me some sort of inner peace. It was calming to know I would see her soon and could make my own judgment about how she was doing. All in all, it was a highly emotional day.

My mother had said a week earlier that her wish was to receive the last rites with the whole family present, so it was decided that this would happen on the weekend that we came. Things weren't looking good, and perhaps she felt the time was nearing.

The days that followed this distressing Sunday before leaving on the following Thursday were, again, extremely worrying. I had my last telephone conversation with my mum on the Tuesday. Although she did her best to make sense, it felt really disturbing. She sounded distant and confused about her illness and kept repeating herself. I decided I wouldn't ring her again because I was to see her on Friday morning. I felt nervous all week, wondering how I would find her this time. The journey on Thursday evening with three boys in the back and my husband there with me driving down the tedious motorway was pleasantly distracting. I had little time and space to think of what was to come. We decided that 9:30 p.m. in the evening was too late to see her, so we checked into our holiday home only three miles from where she lived. I went to bed that night feeling extremely apprehensive about how we would find her in the morning.

Well, finding her the next morning, she did look a lot thinner but still beautiful, with good colour in her face. She was visibly pleased to see us all. Rufus didn't give her his usual cuddle and felt uneasy, most probably sensing that things were different. It soon became apparent that things were different and disturbing.

Mum smiled at the children, who were sitting opposite her in a little row of four (including my husband) on the sofa, but there was no conversation. She was clearly preoccupied and confused about why we had come. She asked, "Why are you here? Am I ill? What is the matter with me?" She appeared to be possessed with the question of why she was ill and what had happened to her. There was a real fear in her eyes and an eagerness to find out why she was ill. Ten seconds after we told her what was the matter, she would ask the same question. Her short-term memory appeared to have totally disappeared. This lady was my mother, but not in the least acting like my mother.

Pete and the boys happily left after about half an hour to do their own thing so I could spend the rest of the day with my mum. I was desperately trying to think of how I could distract her from the everlasting repetitive questions and have some sort of quality time. I went upstairs and got some old photo albums out, which I looked through with her. It did distract her, but the question was still on her lips. At all times, she would try to ask, "What is wrong with me? Am I ill?"

It also became clear that she had lost a lot of memories of events that had happened in the past. I managed to distract her a little for twenty minutes or so. It was so peculiar, and the mother-daughter roles had now been reversed. The expression in her eyes was that of a little girl keen to find the answer to her question, and that expression was there all the time while she was awake. It was disturbing because she didn't understand when I told her that she was ill and had an operation eight months earlier. She often burst out crying, which was the most upsetting. She was like a totally different person. I felt it was so unfair. Why was this happening to her? Her greatest fear in life had always been that she would end up demented in an old-people's home, like her own mother. When she first became ill, she told me that at least that wouldn't happen to her, but on this day, it felt like she was a demented old lady and had become that in the space of only a week. It was heartbreaking. I told her to go to sleep and was relieved when she did because at least when she was lying down with her eyes closed, she looked like my very ill mother rather than my mentally sick mother. It was also a little relief for me because she was so tiring to be with while she was awake.

The phone rang after half an hour and woke her up. She appeared normal and started eating a roll I had left there for her, until she realised she was in a bed and wondered why, which resulted in the same questions. We knew the doctor was coming that afternoon, so we had to stay home. I couldn't think of much distraction to settle her down. One hour with her in this state was exhausting. All I wanted was to have coffee and chat together, or potter around in the garden, but even those simple little things that we had been able to enjoy together were snatched away from us. Me being there must have been such a welcome relief for my siblings.

The doctor finally arrived, and he was also shocked at how quickly she was deteriorating. He suspected that the cancer had gone to her brain and put pressure on it, which resulted in short-term memory loss. He prescribed strong steroids that he hoped would relieve the pressure down and undo the memory loss, at least for a while. He also prescribed something to make her calmer. I went to the chemist soon after, keen to get the tablets so I could have my mum back as soon as possible. The doctor expected to see a difference in her mental state within twenty-four hours. She was given the medication before I said goodbye to her for the day. It was lovely to see my boys and have some sort of normality because the day spent with my mother was so difficult. Having a young family had been a godsend, especially during this phase of my life. All I was craving during this period was normality. But then, what is normality? For me it is being at home with my family during school-time routines and going to bed at night with nothing stressful to apprehend for the next day. Just getting up, sending the kids off to school, cooking dinner, putting the washing on the line, seeing some friends, eating dinner, watching some telly, reading to the kids, having cuddles, having arguments and letting off steam with loved ones, and going to bed. Yes, during these previous nine months, I have realised that it is normality and routine that make me more content than anything else in the world.

JUNE 9
NINE MONTHS AFTER THE DIAGNOSIS

It was decided that with the fast decline in my mother's health and my family from England in Holland, today was the day for my mother's last rites. My brother was keen to cancel because he thought she might panic, but I convinced him to let it go ahead because the doctor had prescribed something to make her calmer. Mum appeared a little less anxious that day, without the real fear in her eyes, but the questions were still possessing her to the same degree as they were the day before.

When I arrived, my sister-in-law, Lion, who had been looking after my mother that morning, had got all her boxes with precious stones out. They were studying them, and I enjoyed joining them. It was another distraction, something my mum had always enjoyed doing. It was half an hour or so of relative normality in the life of my dying mother. We chose some healing stones that were supposed to stop forgetfulness. We put them in a little bag for her to put into her pocket. The half hour of normality soon passed, and the doctor turned up for his daily visit. He was disappointed that the calming medication hadn't made much of a difference to her behaviour but recommended to let the last rites that evening go ahead anyway. He told me how serious the situation was and that it was the right time for the last rites to happen. Later that day, after an exhausting few hours of repetitiveness while trying to keep my mother calm, my sister and I started getting the living room ready for the last-rites ceremony. We placed my mother's chair in the middle of the lounge and surrounded it with chairs, where the rest of her twenty-one-strong family of children and grandchildren would sit.

Mum was confused about the shifting about of the furniture, and I decided to give her a Reiki treatment to try to calm her down. I told her to close her eyes and enjoy the energy coming through, and surprisingly she did. She let it all happen and let me do my work while calmly lying on her bed. She had given me so much healing over the years, and it was time for her to receive now. It made her so much calmer, and at 7:30 p.m., after she had a little sleep, we moved her towards her chair so she would be ready for the rest of the family to arrive for the eight o'clock ceremony. My sister had made the lounge look beautiful, with all my mum's special sculptures visible, as well as a picture of my parents together during happier times, surrounded by candles, flowers, and flower petals. She had blessed the room, creating fresh energy.

When everybody started arriving, Mum was still confused but calm and able to let it all happen. By eight o'clock, the whole family and the priest had arrived, and the mood was somber. My niece started the service off by playing the song "Can You Feel the Love Tonight?" on the piano. There wasn't a dry eye in the room. Every single person present felt the meaning of the words intensely. I was lovingly holding my mother's hand while my sister held the other. The priest continued the service with a joint prayer. He then came up to her to take her hands out of ours and into his and told her how these hands had always been giving in so many ways. My eyes were focused on them. The realisation was more apparent than ever that those were my mother's hands that had loved and cared for me all those years. I knew that soon those hands would be shaped around a clay heart I had made for her to take into eternal life. The priest was preparing my mother's soul for death by giving her the sacrament of the anointing of the sick.

After the formality of the sacrament, we watched a film a close family friend, Lia, had made. It featured things that reminded our friend of my mother, all accompanied by beautiful music. That evening, we all knew and had accepted that the end was nearing. When the last-rites ritual had finished, nobody made any moves to go home. We all stayed in the warmth of my mother's nest. I think she was aware of what had just taken place, and calmness replaced her confusion.

We took her outside in the late-evening sunshine, where she sat in her chair watching the grandchildren play in her garden. She enjoyed watching the children climb the big walnut tree. She looked so content, visibly enjoying being there living in the now, while the sun was setting in the far distance. I wanted it to last forever. Everybody seemed so relieved that the last rites were over and happy to be together with her by our side, knowing all too well that it would be the very last time we would be together in this familiar environment with our beloved mother. We would now be focusing on the end that was nearing. That night, I cried myself to sleep.

I was unaware that the day that followed was going to be the last day I would ever spend with my mother. It was another hot day. When I arrived at her house, she seemed confused again. Diana, my niece, was celebrating her twelfth birthday. I decided to take my mum out in her wheelchair to pick some flowers for Diana in the garden. I had her choose the flowers and let her arrange them in a bouquet. It kept her calm for a while as she gracefully arranged the flowers into a beautiful little posy, which showed that she hadn't lost her ability to be creative. It was calming and therapeutic for her to arrange the flowers, and the focused effort made her forget reality for just a little while. I pushed her wheelchair around the garden again to select one of her smaller sculptures; they were beautifully arranged amongst the flower beds. I helped her choose one for her granddaughter. She picked two little doves that were embracing each other. I think Diana will treasure this little sculpture for the rest of her life. We took our precious gifts over to my brother's house, which was less than a five-minute walk away. About half of the family members were sitting in the garden to celebrate the birthday, and everybody there was surprised but happy to see my mum being wheeled into the garden. Being in a different place, but still surrounded by loved ones, was a good distraction for her. In the back of my mind was the gruelling realisation that at three o'clock, we would have to make our way back to England, and I would have to say goodbye to her again. This time, I had a gut feeling that this was going to be the last time. This was going to be the last time I would see her alive. I wanted to make it special, but three o'clock came around more quickly than I had realised, resulting in a rush to leave and catch the train home.

She was as confused as she had been in the previous few days, and I wasn't sure how to approach saying goodbye this time. It was certainly different than at previous times. I sat next to her and said, "Mum, I'm going back to England now. I've come to say goodbye".

She said, "Yes, I know, but what is the matter with me? Why am I ill?" There was no real content to our parting and she wasn't connecting with me; it felt empty; those last words were meaningless. It didn't feel like I was saying goodbye to my mother. It was a lot easier than the other times when I had to say goodbye. There wasn't the extended eye contact that we had before. She knew I was going back to England, but all she could think about was what was the matter with her. The anxiety was more powerful to her than realising that this was almost certainly going to be the last time we would ever see each other. Should I have said one more "I love you"? No, I feel we had said enough in the last ten months. This goodbye was perhaps emotionless but I was at peace with that. All that mattered was that we both knew that we loved each other. There would always be one more "I love you" that could have been said, no matter what.

My two big boys gave her a hug, and little Rufus lay his head in her lap and stayed like that for about thirty seconds. It was a beautiful moment, and it will be the one I will keep in my memory about this goodbye. My young son was able to capture a pure and intense moment. He was the only one who was able to connect with her properly while she was in this confused and anxious state. It was a symbolic moment that all of us felt.

I will always remember that very last wave of my mother as our car pulled away for the last time from the place I was able to call home in Holland to my home in England. We watched her wave to us through the window from her bed, with my aunt, her sister, sitting next to her. She looked so very thin, especially with both arms up in the air while she was waving at us out for the very last time.

JUNE 11,
WANTING CLOSURE

The day that followed back home in England was empty. I really felt as if I had done my goodbyes now, and I wanted her to die. There was no quality of life left for her. My mother wasn't like my mother anymore. Her brain was affected. Her brain that controlled the being that was my mother had ceased to do the job. I wanted to move on to the next phase. I wanted to start grieving her properly. I craved solace to calm my soul. I felt selfish because I wanted to have my life back. A life of no suitcases, a life where I could plan ahead, a life without waking up and thinking my mother is going to die soon. I was mentally exhausted by saying goodbye to her over and over again, and what happened the previous day felt final to me. I knew it would be better for everybody, including my mother, if she died sooner rather than later.

It was good to be home again. I shared this feeling with my husband that evening, when we sat down for a little relaxing in front of the TV at about nine o'clock. Soon after, my brother Peter rang to tell me that our mother had a really bright moment and she wanted her children to come to her bedside that evening. She was talking sense and told my brothers that she was dying and thanked them for always being there for her. My sister was called, too, and was told to leave work to go and see Mum. She lived half an hour away from my mother's house, but by the time she arrived, Mum had gone back to sleep. I didn't really know how to take this call. Was she going to die tonight? Are they expecting me to take the next boat to the continent to make the long journey back home again? I was pretty upset that they called me at night and decided to stay home.

Nobody knew what was going to happen or when. When she first started being ill, I decided to go and see her once a month, and I decided to stick to that. Later that night, I spoke to my other brother Christian, who had been in England on business when my father died. He understood my dilemma. He told me not to come home because I had only just got back home. He said, "This is a practical problem, and it just can't be helped." It was the confirmation I needed for me to allow myself to think that I had made the right decision to stay home. He also said that for the first time since her illness, he felt that he might have said his final goodbyes, but he treasured that evening and said it was special.

I didn't sleep much that night, thinking she might not make it through the night. I asked my family never to ring me in the night if anything went wrong, so it could have happened and I wouldn't have known. It was a difficult night, and I was half expecting a call early in the morning. In my head, I prepared to leave for Holland. No phone call came, so at 9:00 a.m., I decided to call them. They told me she had had a calm night, she was sleeping a lot, and there was no immediate danger. It was a relief in many ways; it meant I could get on with life at home again, at least for another day. I wasn't planning on ringing my mother because the phone calls, while she was confused, were disturbing and difficult. I had closure now, and if she had died that night, I would have been at peace with that. She hadn't, but everybody was expecting it to happen that week or perhaps the one after that. No quality of life remained for her, and I think we all, including our mother, would have been totally at peace for her to die.

On Thursday, I had an immense feeling of guilt because I "secretly" wanted her to die and had closure, even though she was still alive. I had an immense sudden urge to call her. I needed to talk to her one more time; I needed to hear her voice one more time. I would regret not talking to her for the rest of my life if I didn't ring her, and a sense of guilt would overshadow my life.

I found myself a quiet moment and dialed the number, expecting to be told that she was asleep. The nurse answered and said, "She is awake. Would you like to talk to her?" A nervous ten seconds or so followed, and I was expecting the same confused mother I had said goodbye to on Sunday.

It was against all expectations when she sounded just like my mother: "Hello, Dianne. How are you? So nice to hear your voice." We had a normal conversation, and I burst out in tears. "Mum, you are back! You sound like you again. Do you remember when we saw you over the weekend, and you received your last rites?" I was astonished when she told me that she did. "I remember a lot about the weekend," she said. "I also remember feeling very strange. But I feel better now." We had a short and emotional chat, and I felt elated when I put the phone down. I felt so happy that I had a quality conversation with her, so delighted that she was back in my life and able to talk and act normally. I was able to feel happy again.

I called her again a few days later, and although she sounded like she was mentally stable, she didn't sound so good. She told me that all she did was sleep, and she was too tired to receive visitors. She didn't want other people to come, just her children and direct family. It was just too exhausting. Although I had the feeling that she would quite like to die, I also felt that she was in denial about her illness at that time, blaming the medication for the way she felt. Deep down, she was probably ready to let go but reluctant to let go of her children. That must have been holding her back here a little longer. When I try to imagine letting go of my children, I can totally understand why people want to hold on as long as possible. My mother was a very spiritual person, practicing Reiki and doing meditation on a daily basis, but the hereafter is the unknown and the here is the known. I think it was only natural for her to opt for the known.

JUNE 18
NINE AND A HALF MONTHS AFTER THE DIAGNOSIS–THE CALM

She called me herself, and she sounded really bright and together. It was lovely. She even said that there may be better times ahead when she may be able to go for little walks again. We made some small talk, and it was like the good old times when she was like that. It was a bit of normality that allowed me to have normality in my life. My thirteen-year-old son Luke told me, "Oma is never going to die."

The week that followed was reasonably calm; we talked almost daily. There wasn't much depth to our conversation. Really, the only things we talked about were, "How are you, Mum? How are you feeling? Who came to visit today? What's the weather like? Did you sit outside at all?" And perhaps I would tell her what happened to the children that day. Her life was so very small now, and she was really too tired to make small talk. I always sensed that she tried hard to sound good, to make me feel better. The one thing of great importance she told me that week was that she understood that I had a family to look after in England and that I couldn't be there for her all the time. She told me not to worry about rushing over again while she was relatively stable. She said, "It's OK like this." I got the impression that she would like me to be there for the end, though.

The fact that she told me not to have to be there gave me a little inner peace and took away any feelings of guilt, but still I felt removed from what was really happening over there in Holland. My mother was never really part of my life in England, so things were strangely normal, and nothing was really different, apart from me feeling detached. I felt a bit like an ice queen who was able to put her feelings in the freezer while in the safety of her own home. I think this was happening because I was subconsciously protecting myself and was able to do so while in England because I was physically detached from the situation at home in Holland. I also think that I was able to do this because I was ready to let go of my mother. I had endured almost ten months of saying goodbye to her. It had been a time of love and growth for me. I loved her dearly, but at the end of the day, it is a natural event for someone to lose their parents at some time in their life, and if the parents did their job well and brought their child up to be a stable and secure human being, that person should be able to let go of them. I had reached that stage of being able to let go, and I thank my parents dearly for doing an amasing job.

JUNE 28
ACCEPTANCE
I didn't ring because I felt that Mum was tired the day before and chose not to. My sister called that evening, telling me that Mum was deteriorating quite quickly, needing more morphine due to increased pain, which resulted in her sleeping more. She even chose not to go outside. Her words were, "No, it takes too much effort." My sister told me that Mum seemed to be calm and accepting that she was going to die soon. She told her and my uncle and aunt who were visiting at the time that the angels, my dad, her parents, and her sister who had gone before her would be waiting for her and that she would do her best to give us signs of her presence from the hereafter. She told them to look out for a butterfly.

JUNE 29
SOME FINAL WORDS
I couldn't pluck up the courage to ring again in the morning and decided to call my sister later in the day. It was so much easier to be there and hold her hand, not having to talk but just being there for her and with her. I felt that phoning took too much out of her. At this stage

of her illness, all I could do for her was send her Reiki because phoning was getting more and more frustrating and emotionally difficult for both of us. My sister told me that Mum's health was declining quite fast. The doctor visited her that morning, and due to excessive pain, he prescribed still more morphine. One of my brothers made the decision to call me to give me the option to come over because things seemed to deteriorate. But gladly, my sister told him that I had said my goodbyes so many times and that I had decided to stay home for now. My sister and I talked and imagined how the end would evolve. We were both of the opinion that it would be nice if Mum just quietly went in the night.

I rang later, knowing that Mum wouldn't pick up the phone, and spoke to the nurse, Maria, who was looking after her. I asked her to pass on a message to my mum from me. "Tell her that I love her very much and that it's OK to let go now." A few hours later, I called Maria again and asked if she had a chance to pass on the message to her. She had. My mother had told her to tell me that she knew I loved her and that she loved me very much, too. She also told her that she wanted me to know that she was aware that she was very much in my thoughts and how difficult it was for me with a young family to come over. She said she knew I had done my very best to support her in the best possible way during her illness, for which she was very grateful. It was a relief to me that we had been able to exchange these loving messages, even though it was through a third party. It would have been a lot harder if I had communicated with her directly, not only because she was so frail, but speaking of love for each other through the telephone would have been emotional, and I would have felt a sense of frustration not being by her side to hold her hand. This exchange of messages felt to me like the final communication between us, and it surprised me that I was so at peace with that.

The nurse, Maria, who over the months had become a great support and friend to my mother, also told me that Mum's pulse was shallow and that she had had little to drink that day. Of course nobody knew when she was going to die, but Maria told me that her shallow breathing could be an indicator of imminent death. Maria also believed that she was at peace and had given in to the fact that death was just around the corner. That meant that, without any resistance, it was now just a matter of time. It gave me a sense of calm knowing that Maria was looking after her that night. She had returned that day from a six-week holiday. Perhaps my mother had chosen to wait for her return so she could be with her in the night, as she had been there with her through many dark nights when she had calmed and guided my mother with her wisdom and knowledge. That evening, I sent my mother Reiki healing. While doing this, I felt deeply connected with her. It was my way of being there for her in spirit. If this was going to be the night of her death, I knew that the Reiki would help her make a calm transition between life and death. I went to bed that night feeling emotional but calm. I told my brothers and sister not to ring me until the morning if she died during the night.

6

Mum's Final Goodbye

NINE MONTHS AND THREE WEEKS AFTER THE DIAGNOSIS

It was 8:30 a.m., and I hadn't heard anything, so I was pretty certain that Mum was still alive. I chose to delay the difficult task of ringing home, choosing instead the easy task of making pancakes for the boys, as we traditionally do every Saturday morning. It was the usual morning mayhem, Henry was about to be picked up to go for a taster day at his new secondary school, I was about to clean the holiday let, our eldest boy Luke was still in bed, my husband was relaxing outside while watering the plants, Rufus was squeezing too much maple syrup onto his pancakes. The phone rang. It stopped me in my tracks, and I felt anxiety pumping through my body. I knew it was a call from Holland, and in my head all sorts of scenarios of how the day would continue unfolded in a matter of seconds. I picked up the phone, and at the other end was my eldest brother, Peter. He never rings for a chitchat, so immediately I knew it was something important. He told me that our mother was deteriorating fast and that she would almost certainly die in the next few days. He felt that I should know so I could start planning my trip home. I thanked him. As soon as I put down the phone, my brain went crazy with different options and choices I had to make. *What do I do? Go now? Rush over? Wait a day?* My thoughts were interrupted after a few minutes when a parent came to pick up Henry. I let him go. He would be back at one o'clock, and it gave me

166

a little bit more space, with one less child in the house, to get my act together. Everything happening at that time was just focused on when and how I would be going to Holland. There was no space to reflect and think. I went online to see if I could book the Eurostar to Brussels and go on from there, taking my oldest son, Luke. But no trains were leaving from Ashford that day. The only other option was to take the car over, but then really we should take the whole family with us. I felt it seemed sensible to all go over early on Sunday morning. That gave me time to get my act together.

As I was planning the logistics and the travelling, only forty minutes after my brother's first phone call, the phone rang again. Anxiety kicked in immediately. The same voice came through the line. My brother, Peter, didn't have to say anything after his initial "Hello, Dianne."

I asked, "Did she die?"

He said, "Yes, she has just died. Your brother and sister didn't get here on time either. It all went quickly and lasted only about one and a half minutes. A few breaths, and she was gone."

I said, "She really has died? She's gone?" I started crying and asked him again the same question. After another confirmation from my brother, I said goodbye to him and hung up the phone. I had been preparing for this moment for ten long months. Nobody knew that June 30, 2012 would be the day my mother was going to die. My mother's race for life was over, and now that the finish was confirmed, it still felt like an earthquake had hit me. I felt confused, tearful, emotional, and erratic. I went to find Pete in the garden. He gave me a big hug, and I could tell that this was also a big loss to him. I was so glad he had the day off that day. He soon retreated back to his plants, which is his way of dealing with any emotional or problematic issues. My thirteen-year-old son, Luke, isolated himself in his back-garden studio space to let the news sink in. I went to see him half an hour later, and he told me to leave him alone. It was out of character for him, but he seemed upset and angry and wanted me to give him privacy and space.

Two-year-old Rufus felt something was up but couldn't quite put his finger on it. He had been talking about Oma going to heaven for some time, and for now he was at peace with the fact that she had finally gone there, with not too many further questions.

Henry, my middle boy, would not find out until later. I felt that, rather than running off to Holland in a rush, we should let the news sink in. So we decided to go all together as a family on Sunday morning. I wanted to keep my boys and husband close to me because I knew that the comfort of being together would ease the pain for all of us.

I spent most of the day packing, a huge job that was comparable to going on a family holiday, the only difference being the type of clothes to take and the emotions attached. I had to cancel all the business for the coming week, book travel tickets, and reserve a self-catering cottage to stay in. It was a huge job that kept me busy most of the day, but there were moments when I stopped and reflected, moments when I stopped to think about my mother. They occurred when I stumbled across things that associated me with her. I had many clothes that my mother had given me while she was ill because they didn't fit her anymore. I would pick up garments that had changed from a piece of clothing to a piece of my mother that carried emotional value. The scent reminded me of her, and it made me realise that these clothes would be a way of recapturing her scent. I would also have these instances when I came across the many sculptures made by her hands, most of them personalised in the theme of love in some way or another. I realised how precious these sculptures would be from now on, and it made me see even more what a beautiful person she was. These moments led to quiet little bouts of crying and reflection throughout that day.

I told the news of my mother's death to my good friend, Ria, in Holland and one local friend in England who would inform the school and the neighbours who were going to look after the chickens while we were away, but otherwise I kept the news quiet all day. I couldn't physically cope with any phone calls because I just didn't have time until I put Rufus to bed at seven o'clock, and the car was packed ready for the big day that was to come. When that time finally came, I went for a walk through the garden and made myself sit on a bench, where I could reflect on what had happened and let the news of my mother's death sink in a little. It was so peaceful to just sit there for a while, thinking this could be a time of quiet to listen and look for signs from her. She had told me she would show me signs of her presence if she possibly could. I found myself looking up at the sky, like I did when my father died and wondering where she was. I didn't sense presence from my mother in any shape or form. While I sat there, I realised that the parting of my mother from this world seemed a lot more significant than when the umbilical cord was severed when I entered this world. Perhaps I should visualise the umbilical cord being reconnected in a new configuration where we can't see each other. Just like before I was born, when I was unknowingly connected.

While thinking about all these new theories, my oldest son, Luke, came looking for me, as he always does, and I told him I needed a bit of time alone. He went away and picked me some gooseberries, which we shared. Earlier that day, when I told him his Oma died, he had taken it quite badly and was upset. I told him how he always had been special to Oma and that she wouldn't want to see him sad or angry about what had happened. It was nice to share a special moment with him, eating gooseberries on the bench. When I told my Rufus, who was almost three, that morning that Oma had gone to heaven, he asked me where heaven was. I told him, "It's somewhere near the stars, and it's very nice there." He thought there must be cars there if it's nice. He was particularly cuddly and easy to manage that day, as if he knew. I think little ones are so intuitive. Henry, my middle son, who was ten, acted calmly. He went out for a jog and was generally quiet all day. They were all prepared for this day and had been to Holland to say their goodbyes about three times since Mum fell terminally ill. Their lives had also been on hold somewhat in the previous ten months. I would often tell them, "Sorry, but I can't plan ahead because Oma is going to die soon!" I think they had mixed feelings of sadness but also relief about this day.

My time on the bench led to another walk through the garden with my husband, where we talked about how he felt about losing his mother-in-law and how he felt her presence through all the plants and flowers she had given to us over the years. He thought she was a thoughtful person who always looked after him and cared for him. It was a big loss to him, too. We had a giggle about her speciality dish, "rabbit stew," which she tried to impress him with when he first met my parents and which he really disliked.

The day brought us closer together as we remembered my mum while the sun was setting above our little church.

Later that evening, I got around to texting my friends, telling them what happened. I asked them not to ring until after I got back in five days, on Thursday. I was too exhausted and just wanted to collapse in front of the TV with a glass of wine. We watched Tim Henman win at Wimbledon and took ourselves to bed around midnight. The alarm was set for 5:30 a.m., when another day full of emotions would begin.

JULY 1

We got away as planned, and I felt surprisingly normal and OK. I was glad the car was all packed up so all I had to do was make some bacon rolls to enjoy on our journey and get the boys out of bed and into the car. I had to compose myself when I routinely walked to the phone to let my mother know when we set off and what time we were due to arrive. Today I realised that nobody really cared when we arrived anymore, nor would anybody worry about our journey being a safe one. I expected and hoped that my sister would take over that role. I anticipate that we will fill in some of this void that has been created by our mother dying.

We were quite happily travelling along on the Belgium motorway when the song "Sing," the Queen's Jubilee song, reminding me of my mum when she was sick, played on the radio. I started crying uncontrollably, even though I knew my mother would want me to sing and be happy. As before, I found myself looking up at the sky, wondering where she had gone, with my eyes fixed on the ever-changing, graceful, white clouds, all in the exact colour of my mother's white-silver hair. One of the clouds appeared to be in the shape of her head, and I wanted to believe that this cloud was perhaps a sign from my mother. I allowed myself the comfort of that belief. I was in control of my own thoughts, and nobody would judge me for them. They resulted in something that was a welcome release of emotions.

As we got closer to Holland, I was starting to get more and more anxious about arriving home, where I had to face my mother's dead body. My previous experience of coming home when my father died had occupied my mind for quite some time. I remembered the moment of walking into the house and not being welcomed by a parent who loves me unconditionally. The realisation of that loss is at its most challenging when you walk into their space and they're not there anymore.

Walking into my mother's house without my mother there, without her soul present, only her dead body, was difficult. I couldn't prepare for that or anticipate what my feelings would be. All I knew was that it was going to be very emotional. But it had to be done. I couldn't run away from it. I also knew that once that moment had passed, I would feel some kind of inner peace. In the final ten miles of our journey, as we approached her house, anxious thoughts took control of me. When we arrived, I was relieved to see my brothers' and sister's cars. They all wanted to be there to offer me support when I arrived home. They were waiting for me inside, and I knew that I couldn't delay the reality of going in any longer. I opened the door, and an emotional welcome home followed. The embraces with my siblings were so comforting in sympathy with each other and our shared loss. Within seconds of setting foot in the door, everything felt OK, and I was in the very place that I belonged at that very time.

My mother's body was laid to rest in her bedroom, which gave us as a family the opportunity to say goodbye to her at any given moment if we chose to do so. Seeing dead people isn't one of my strengths and is something I avoid if I possibly can, but I felt I had to see my mother as a sign of my respect for her.

I didn't cherish seeing my father in his coffin; it was very upsetting for me. The image of him lying in his coffin haunts me sometimes. I like to remember people how they were, not how they looked dead, lying in a coffin.

My brothers and sister had decided that my mum wouldn't lie in her coffin but instead in her bed until the day of her funeral. They made the atmosphere in her bedroom as beautiful as possible. They told me there was peaceful music, with candles, flowers, and her loving sculptures surrounding her. My sister, Ans, who believed that being with her body was something healing and beautiful, prepared me before I went into Mum's bedroom to see her. Ans told me to take my time in Mum's room and to really make contact with her instead of making it rushed. She said I needed to allow myself some time to relax, go up close to her face, and look at her as she lay in total peace. She assured me that if I did that, I would be OK. My sister was succeeding in calming me, and after a few minutes, I felt mentally prepared and ready to go in.

Ans opened the door. It felt like I was entering a beautiful temple, with the gentle glow of candles and the calming sound of meditation music. Mum was surrounded by her sculptures and everything she loved that was beautiful and meaningful to her. It was extremely peaceful, and my mother looked like a goddess. She wore her beautiful red dress she had bought only recently for Queens Day, and had so much joy in wearing. She wore her angel necklace that a friend gave her for extra strength and help. From a distance, she looked old and frail, but when I got closer to her face, she looked at peace and beautiful. The skin on her face was smooth and brown against her beautiful white angel hair.

You could tell by the expression on her face that she had made a peaceful passing only twenty-four hours earlier. I finally felt calm and quietly sat there by her side. My sister left me and Pete to be with her on our own. We talked about how grateful we had been to her for everything she had done for us. After another five minutes, Pete left so I could be on my own with her. I surprised myself and somehow did cope on my own, although it felt quite surreal. There I was, sitting with my mother. Never before had it felt unusual and eerie to be with her in my life until now, when she was dead. I did want to touch her before I said goodbye but was reluctant because I was fearful of feeling the coldness of her body. Instead, I stroked her beautiful hair gently and said, "Thank you for being a good mother." That filled me with unconditional love. I blew her a kiss goodbye and knew that it would be the last time I would see this beautiful familiar face.

That afternoon, we had to get to work on preparing the funeral. In Holland, it's compulsory to bury a person within three working days, so there was a lot to do to prepare the funeral. My brothers, sister, and I had a little meeting in which we gave each other tasks. There was no time to really grieve—just planning. We all wanted the most beautiful service for our mother in an ambience that would suit her taste and personality. There was so much to organise. My sister Ans and I yet again had the task of writing a eulogy to be printed on the back of Mum's photograph to be handed out to all the guests at the funeral. We isolated ourselves in our mother's meditation room, as we did when our father had died. The words came freely, and this is what we wrote.

Flowers and nature were part of you. Hydrangeas, a dahlia, a tulip, or a red rose; our mother knew the beauty of every flower. She loved being among the flowers. She picked them, she arranged them, and she passed them on.

People to her were like flowers. "They are all different and all beautiful" was a well-known phrase she used to say. Our mother was gifted in the art of connecting, of being part of the whole. By doing this, she managed to create a close-knit family. During her whole life, she would be there for people who needed help—not just her family, but also friends, neighbours, and anybody who needed support. In this way, she showed and taught us that we are all connected.

We children and grandchildren have always experienced that she embraced us all being different. She made us believe in ourselves, gave us a sense of security and belonging, but above all, she gave us a very warm nest to which all our friends were welcome, too. She gave us the space to make our own decisions and to follow our hearts.

She spoke with the power of "It's the small things in life that matter most." A card, a bunch of flowers, a present whose wrapping would be a gift in itself. Creating was important to her. Through this, she expressed her feelings, also during difficult times in her life. This creating was mainly done through making sculptures, many of which she gave away. Through these pieces of art, she will always keep being a visible part in our lives.

In the past few years, most of her sculpture creations were angels, Mother's last one being that of Archangel Michael, who symbolises the Prince of Light, who conquers the demons of darkness and celebrates the coming of light.

Through her strength and positivity, her last phase of life was still very much worth living. She enjoyed it, and with this the circle of life became complete.

Mum, thank you! You made our lives whole.

The family would like to thank you for sharing and being there for Toos during her illness and at the funeral in your own special way.

The rest of the day was spent with family and friends popping in and out with hugs, flowers, memories but also with relief about the fact our mother was released of her suffering. Some would go and see my mother and my siblings would take it in turn going in her bedroom with our guests as easy as if they would pop off to the kitchen to get a glass of water. I couldn't understand how it was effortless for them and not for me. The mood certainly wasn't sad while everybody was busy talking and organising. It was such a great contrast with what lied behind my mother's bedroom door in the very same house. That evening as all my family settled down in the garden we treated ourselves to a Chinese takeaway and enjoyed being together. We reminisced while the sun was setting on another beautiful summer's day.

That night, I went to bed totally exhausted.

JULY 2
PREPARING THE FUNERAL

Up early, my sister picked me up at ten o'clock for another busy day of organising, with no real time to grieve.

Our first call was at a friend's house. He is a musician, and my mother used to go to him for singing lessons. He was only too happy to be involved in my mother's funeral service, and it didn't take long before the music was falling into place. We chose a serene mantra that would be sung as my mother entered the church. He was also going to accompany us on the piano during our solo, "When the Night Becomes Dark," a song from the Taize community. It felt so nice to feel that things were starting to fall into place.

Back home, though, there were some tensions due to different opinions about which content to put into the funeral service and which to put into the wake. After some harsh words, to be expected when tension is high, we came to a mutual agreement, and it was decided that the daughters (my sister and I) would take care of the funeral, and the boys (my three brothers) would organise the wake. In normal circumstances, it would have been my mother who would have calmed things down and settled the argument. It was confrontational. We all realised that from now on, we had to smooth things out by ourselves. No more parent to manage any sibling rivalry.

At the end of that day, things were really starting to take shape, and we all thought it was justified to order another Chinese takeaway, which we enjoyed, just like the night before in my mum's garden. The weather was smashing, and we needed to wind down at the end of the day with some lightness and laughter. We decided that it would be a healing activity for the children and possibly for the parents to write a little message to Oma on the inside of her coffin lid. That evening, we placed it on the grass in the garden with some colouring in pens so the children and adults could write a message for my mum on the inside of the lid. Rufus drew a picture of him and her accompanied, of course, by a car. When I told him it was the lid of the box that would take Oma into heaven, he also wanted to draw a hot-air balloon, presumably to help her get there. Everybody wanted to get involved, and it ended up with lots of colourful messages. It was a nice thought to visualise that the messages would be close to my mother when the coffin was sealed, especially for the children among us.

We ended the evening with my brother, Peter, reading the kind words about my mother in the condolence cards we received. Reading these caring and lovely words about our mother out loud was emotional for him but also for us. The ones we enjoyed reading most were the ones that said something specific about my mother or told how she had made a difference to somebody's life. She was our mother and had shaped our lives. But she had also made a difference to many other people as well, and her life had been one worth living. With that nice thought, we all took ourselves off to bed.

JULY 3
SOME TIME TO REFLECT

We decided that this day would be a rest day, and we gave ourselves a day off with our own little families. Finally some time to reflect. I woke up early again and was keen for this week to be over as I knew that there would be no inner peace for me until my mother was buried. I was apprehensive about the wake and the funeral, not knowing how I would feel, but on the other hand I wanted to give my mum the best send-off ever. She deserved it.

Before the rest of the family woke up, I chose to pick a moment of peace and quiet and just sit outside our holiday house for a bit of thinking and to look out for signs of her presence. After all, she had told us to watch out and feel for signs. Sadly, again, I didn't feel her spirit—just nothing.

It didn't take long for the rest of the family to wake up, and we decided to enter into a bit of normality and all do some shopping in my little hometown, although I was desperately hoping not to bump into anybody I knew. I wanted to be left alone and have privacy. When we were pushing our shopping trolley through the local supermarket, I suddenly burst into tears. The realisation hit me that I would never go shopping with my mum again. I felt a lot of emotional pain and was surprised to fall to pieces there and then. I just wanted to go back to our little holiday house. On our way back to the car, I bumped into an old school friend. She had already read on Facebook about my mother's death and gave me a big hug. I didn't need to explain, and I enjoyed the hug.

When we got back to the holiday house, I lay in the sun for a while, just doing nothing and being with my family. We had to go back to my mum's house by six o'clock to prepare for the wake at seven. The wake in Holland is a service that is held the day before the funeral. It gives adults and children the opportunity to say goodbye if they are unavailable to come to the funeral. It's a bit like a minifuneral service without a dead body present, which makes the event somewhat lighter. We all gathered at the house, and I could sense some nerves. We were all anticipating the final goodbye, which would take place in eighteen hours or so. All the family took the five-minute walk to church together, and somehow it felt wrong to leave my mother's body alone in the house. I felt a real responsibility and natural need for her to come. It was such an unexpected emotion, and I wasn't quite sure how to deal with it. I realised that until she was buried, she would remain to be the center of my concerns.

The service was emotional, and I cried a lot. My brothers chose some beautiful pieces of music that reminded me of her. One that was played at the end of the service was "Time to Say Good-Bye" by Andrea Bocelli. I had many memories of this song, from a period in my parents' life about ten years earlier, when they used to play this music frequently. It provoked a surge of emotional release. The service had turned out beautifully and was well attended. Many old friends and family were there waiting after the service outside the church to greet and hug us. All who attended the wake service in the church were invited to see my mother's body if they wished to do so. A queue of about twenty-five people lined up outside her house, quietly waiting their turn to pay their last respects and say their final farewell.

When the viewing had finished and friends and family had all gone home, the time came where all us children were going to have our final goodbye and farewell, followed by the closure of her coffin, as we had done with our father. I chose to protect myself and told them that I couldn't do it this time as I didn't feel that it was helping me at all, even on a deeper level. I had said my goodbyes when I had spent time alone with her body and that for me was our final time together. I could not face seeing her dead again. I asked my sister if she would put the clay heart I made with my mum in the coffin. I wrote "love never dies" on it. When we made it together about five months earlier

I knew then that it would end up with her in her resting place. When my siblings had gone in to close the coffin it felt to me that they took a very long time and it gave me unwanted time to question my decision of not joining them. I know it was unjust to think it, but at that time I felt like the black sheep of the family a little bit. I was relieved to see them all back and my sister told me that she placed the heart in her hands which was just as I had envisaged and I was grateful to her. With that moving image of my mother holding the clay heart in her hands in the coffin I left my mother's house that evening. She would hold my heart forever.

4TH JULY
DAY OF THE FUNERAL

I woke early again that morning, mindful of the fact that it was the day of my mother's funeral. A time that any human being dreads and that comes around only once in a life time. That day, beautiful warm and sunny, the July 4, 2012 it was my turn to bury my beloved mother. While the rest of the family were still asleep I took the opportunity to sit in the quiet little garden surrounding our holiday house and spent some time listening to all the normalities of daily life in the distance. Dustcarts, cars driving to work, birds going about their usual business, while in my head I was visualising the day ahead when I was going to say farewell to my mother. Today it would be me in that funeral parlour and people would be looking at me in sorrow. Tuning into the sounds of normality made me realise that soon I would become part of day to day society again, something that had been lacking somewhat in the last ten months.

I decided that I was going to embrace the day and make it beautiful for my mother. I wanted to make her proud of her children just in case she was looking down from above.

I felt together and focused that morning and got the whole family ready and in the car early and calmly. Nerves set in as we approached my mother's village. The funeral was at 10:30 a.m., so we decided to all meet at her place at 9:45 a.m. As we turned into her street anxious thoughts were creeping in about the day ahead and when the house became visible so did the hearse. The sight of it made everything seem real and really happening. It wouldn't be long now before my mother's coffin would be in that hearse with the confrontational reality that she would be leaving her beloved house for the last time and that we children would lose our parental home for good.

We parked our car on the green, and when we got inside the house, everybody had arrived. There was a light atmosphere with my siblings, nephews, nieces, and in-laws busying themselves with taking the flowers outside and making sure they all looked in tip-top shape. As with every event, there were last-minute details that had to be addressed and it made the mood virtually excitable. The coffin was ready and waiting in the hallway, ready to be taken out through the front door. The time had come to show two-year-old Rufus the coffin and tell him that Oma was in there, ready to go to heaven. He was more interested in the trolley with wheels it was standing on than in the coffin and content; so for now I was relieved that I had no more explaining to do.

The coffin was white and had the most beautiful pink flower arrangement on it, lovingly made by my mother's sister, Nell, who is a florist. My brothers were gathering in the hall too, ready to take the coffin into the hearse. All of a sudden the family started to go quiet and all, with the exception of my brothers, went outside gathering on the green where many cars with guests in were arriving for the funeral. Friends and family waved from a distance choosing to leave us in privacy while my mother's body was taken out of her house for the very last time. It was emotional watching my brothers wheeling the coffin out of the house while the grandchildren lined both sides of the path leading up to the hearse holding flowers. It crossed my mind, having three sons of my own, that one day they might do the same for me. I stood very close to my sister and although my eyes were fixed onto the coffin I found her hand as we both watched mum leave her house for the very last time. My brothers gently lifted the coffin into the hearse. The doors to the hearse were closed by a funeral director. The family gathered behind the hearse from different angles and watched it very slowly drive away. Our beloved mother and grandmother surrounded by a sea of flowers was driven off to the church. The children were hugging their parents and tears were starting to flow.

We chose not to walk behind the hearse and made the five-minute walk to church by ourselves, leaving just after the hearse was out of sight. We walked close together united as a family, and just like when we walked our father to church for his burial, the bell tower of the church rang its somber funeral tune. Locals stopped what they were doing out of respect for the family and gave us polite quiet nods. The big difference this time though was that we walked without a supporting parent by our side. As of today we were the senior generation and our own imminent mortality was undeniable. A realisation that is only really fully felt when both parents have died.

When we arrived at the church, my sister, Pete, the sister-in-laws, and I decided not to enter behind the coffin. Instead, we chose to go ahead because all the rest of the family had tasks such as carrying the coffin, and the children were bringing in the flowers. My sister and I had to get ready by the piano to start singing the mantra when the coffin entered the church. When we opened the church door, we saw that it was packed, which was comforting. All of these people came out of respect for my mother. As we walked the long aisle, I felt curious eyes following us all the way down to our seats in the second row. We sat there quietly awaiting the time for the coffin to enter and listening to the beautiful music that our friend was playing. I knew that the next hour and a half would probably be one of the most important and memorable events in my life. I could hear people standing up at the back of the church and knew the time had come for my mother's body to enter the church. My sister and I made our way to the nearby piano and looked towards the back of the church. There she came, carried by my brothers and nephew, and preceded by the grandchildren holding the flowers. Our friend started playing the music of the mantra, and my sister and I started singing: "May the blessings of love be upon you, may your soul abide with you, may the spirit illuminate your heart, now and forevermore."

Slowly but surely, more friends and family joined in with the singing of the mantra, and the sound and intensity became stronger while the coffin was slowly carried down the aisle. You could feel the church swelling with love. It was so very beautiful, gentle, and moving. By the time she had reached the altar, the energy in the church was astounding. Everybody there meant the words they were singing, and the love for her shone through this voice of unity. It was a powerful moment. This mantra had a lot of meaning to my mother because friends in her choir group had sung it to her during her illness. The meaning of the words and the music accompanying it had touched her deeply.

The service lasted an hour and a half, and it was a true celebration of her life. Her white coffin was surrounded by candles, flowers, and her sculptures. My sister and I sang another song together from the depths of our hearts, during which we managed to hold ourselves together. This was the last tribute. She was always so proud of her children, and I certainly wanted her to be proud on that day. The service was feminine, just like she was, and it was so clear that my mother was loved by so many. At the end of the service, I read the following poem:

In beauty may I walk.
All day long may I walk.
Through the returning seasons may I walk.
On the trail marked with pollen may I walk.
With grasshoppers about my feet may I walk.
With dew about my feet may I walk.
With beauty may I walk.
With beauty before me, may I walk.
With beauty behind me, may I walk.
With beauty above me, may I walk.
With beauty below me, may I walk.
With beauty all around me, may I walk.

In old age wandering on a trail of beauty, lively, may I walk.
In old age wandering on a trail of beauty, living again, may I walk.
It is finished in beauty.
It is finished in beauty.

I read it calmly and beautifully, and again the words came straight from the heart. It felt so effortless to say these words, wishing my mother only beauty and love on her journey. The poem was followed by the mantra that was sang when she entered the church. The congregation quietly sang along while the priest was blessing the coffin with incense and prayers. The energy in the church was loving, with the sound of quiet cries while people remembered my serene and graceful mother.

My brothers and 20 year old nephew slowly walked over to the coffin, lifted it onto their shoulders, and started walking down the aisle. My sister and I followed directly behind, holding hands and singing the mantra with the rest of the church. We felt strong together, walking behind her coffin. As we left the church, we were met by the warm summer air. We continued to make our way to the back of the church, where her final resting place was going to be while the church bells struck twelve o'clock. This familiar childhood sound of the church clock tower, which I used to listen to from my bedroom when I was a child, together with the congregation singing the mantra inside the church, was extraordinary and beautiful. When we reached the churchyard, we waited at the side of the coffin and watched the rest of the congregation slowly making their way to her final resting place—my mother's family, friends, neighbours, and people I didn't know but knew her and cared for her. They all walked around the coffin saying their final goodbyes, some touching the coffin, some making a little bow, and some saying their own private little messages while pausing at the top of the grave. As they walked away, a few made eye contact with us, her children, showing us sympathy, love, and strength with their eyes.

It took about fifteen minutes for everybody to pay their final respects in their own unique and welcoming way until it was just my brothers and sister, our partners, and the grandchildren by her side. We all circled the coffin and held hands. We took a moment of quiet time, each of us thinking our own private thoughts. Rufus was given a white, heart-shaped balloon, which he let go of. We watched it disappear into the sky. It was a moment of symbolism that Oma's soul was slowly moving away from us toward heaven. It gave all of us a sense of closure as we watched the balloon disappear up into the blue heavens, and it made it easier to see the coffin being lowered into my dad's grave, where their bodies would rest together. We all paid our last respects and left the churchyard together. I felt relieved and very much at peace walking away from their grave, knowing their bodies had been reunited and that my mother's spirit had been set free and relieved. I also felt relieved to know that my life could finally move forward again. These last ten months had not been a time of empty steps, and I was very aware that I had grown more as a person than I would have in normal circumstances. It had been a time of more shade than light. You can't avoid sad times in life. You have to feel those dark times to be able to experience happiness. I felt, when walking away from the churchyard, that lighter times were just around the corner. The grief would cast a shadow, although having gone through these past months made me appreciate what I did have left in my life so much more.

We joined our family and friends at the village venue for lunch, where people had the opportunity to express their condolences to us. It was a lovely reunion of family and friends, and I enjoyed the stories of my mother that were told that afternoon while being bathed in the hot July sunshine.

After that memorable afternoon, we decided we would all meet that evening at my mum's house for yet another meal together. We all were aware that being together in this familiar place called home was coming to an end. It was another beautiful evening that we spent in her garden. The relief I felt was clearly also felt by the rest of the family.

We could all move on into the next phase of our lives that had been a long time coming—a life without parents.

While enjoying the evening, my sister and I thought it was a good idea to water the flowers on our parents' grave. As we made our walk to the churchyard, we decided to really try and feel when we got there. We stood in front of the grave and decided to close our eyes. After about twenty seconds, I felt dizzy and experienced a real sense of two waves of energy—the energy of both my father and my mother. It was a beautiful moment, a gift from our parents telling us all was OK and that they were reunited. I felt these energies wrapping like a plait around my body—two strands: one of my father and the other of my mother. I felt dizzy and overwhelmed by love. It lasted for a few minutes, and it made me happy. It confirmed that all was OK. When I opened my eyes, my sister looked at me in anticipation of my reaction. She had had an amazing similar experience. It confirmed for me that this sensation was real, and it made a contented ending to this memorable day.

AFTER THE FUNERAL

The weeks following the funeral back home were emotional. There were so many emotional triggers everywhere I looked and went, including all the beautiful sculptures she had made. There are probably at least three sculptures in every room of the house and many more in the garden. Seeing them made me want to touch them. I would place my fingers on them and trace their shapes, just like my mother's hands had done in the years gone by. I would feel an affectionate connection doing this while closing my eyes.

Another trigger was music, especially while driving the car. It was the only private place where I couldn't be seen and where the music would evoke memories while tears could flow.

At bedtime, Rufus and I would often talk about Oma while listening to the music coming out of the music box that she had given him. He asked many questions about heaven, and I tried to answer them in a satisfying way. He would often run in full of excitement with a white feather in his little hand that he found outside, delighted to be sent another little sign from up in the heavens. He was a great healing influence for all the family.

It was often true that when with friends the realisation that the unconditional love of my parents had gone was more confrontational and tough. Friends would talk about their parents in the present tense while I could only join in by talking about mine in the past tense. When my mother was ill I could still join in on conversations in current tense but now she had also passed away both of my parents were something of the past.

On numerous occasions I instinctively picked up the phone to ring my mother only to realise that I couldn't. On the Sunday after the funeral I tried to ring my sister because I felt the need to talk. We did after all share the same loss. She didn't pick up the phone so I tried to call all three of my brothers. None of them were home. I concluded that they had probably all met at my mother's house again. *How dare they*, I thought, *without me*. So I decided to call my mother's number with the expectation that the phone would be picked up. Dialling her familiar number felt like such a nice and everyday thing to do. This nice feeling was soon to be contrasted by a gruelling feeling when I realised that the phone line was dead. The long tone of disconnection on the other side of the line turned out to be a low moment in my journey of grief. The phone had been my main source of communication, and when she died, that way of communicating had died with her. But the fact that I couldn't even ring the number with anticipation that it may be picked up was difficult for me. Perhaps it was a good thing that the line had been cut off because it took away the opportunity of trying to ring her over and over again with no reply, which would have probably upset me on numerous occasions in the future.

It turned out that all my siblings were doing their own individual things, too, dealing with their grief in their own private ways. I was feeling quite vulnerable. Most people will agree that part of the grieving is best done on your own. Finding solace with others just delays the journey through the dark tunnel that everybody has to travel, partly on their own, before finding the light again.

Two weeks after the funeral, the boys started their seven-week summer break, so there was not much time to be alone and reflect during this time. On top of the mayhem caused by the kids, we were also having a six-month major extension done to our house, requiring daily decisions, money spent, and endless coffee for the builders. The months following my mother's death were disorganised, stressful, and restless. The children needed attention and entertaining and needed to be taken here, there, and everywhere. My life was yet again hectic and mad.

In the third week of the Summer holiday, we went back to Holland. Some formalities with regard to my mother's will needed to be addressed, and we were having a meeting with my brothers and sister about what to do with my mother's estate. My mother's house was unoccupied with all her belongings still in it, so it made sense for us to stay there, even though it meant driving to her house without her and her love there to greet us. The last time I visited when she was still alive, although gravely ill and confused, she was happy to see me, and even then I felt the unconditional love through and through. Knowing that my mother wasn't going to be there for our next visit meant that yet again I had to prepare for an emotional journey and homecoming, this time on a completely different level. I took the children with me and was quite happy driving on my usual journey through Belgium. As usual, the children were successful in the art of distraction. When we crossed the border from Belgium into Holland, the tears soon emerged. Usually at that part of the journey, I would be preparing to see my mum, looking in the mirror to check if my hair looked OK, telling the boys to behave when we got there, and imagining how our visit would be. This time, I was preparing for a Dutch life without a mother. During the final ten minutes of our journey, I was having challenging visions of my mother cycling on her bike and making her daily walk through the village. I was imagining elderly ladies on bicycles to look like my mother, but of course the reality was that they weren't her. I would never see her on her bike or on her walks again.

The boys noticed that I was crying quietly, and my middle boy, Henry, tried to make me feel better by saying, "Mummy, Oma is not suffering anymore, so perhaps it's good that she died." My children don't like it when I cry, and it melts my heart when they say or do things to try and make me feel better. I didn't hide my tears from them because I felt it was important that I expressed my sadness to them. It was giving them the opportunity to help me through my grief as well as their own. If I had hidden my feelings, I would have taken away the opportunity for them to share our joined grief. Every human being has to learn loss at some point in their lives, and by letting my children see my pain, I was setting an example that crying is OK, and sadness is real. It's an emotion I wanted them to embrace and feel, too. By accepting this pain and living the loss, we were creating space for new harmony and acceptance and a chance to move on in our lives.

When we arrived at the house, there was nobody to greet us. My brother had told me where the key was hidden. It seemed bare, and I felt a deep void when we got out of the car. I knew I had to just get on with it. So I bravely unlocked and opened the door. As soon as we set foot in the door, the house alarm went off. It abruptly put my emotions on the back burner because I didn't know the code to switch it off. After about fifteen minutes of frustration and crushed emotion, I finally got in touch with one of my brothers, who soon came to the rescue. Perhaps the alarm was a blessing in disguise! It is quite amazing how life can bring you so many different emotions in such a small amount of time and how it has the ability to jump from one reality to another.

That evening, when the children were in bed and I was alone in my mother's familiar house with all her belongings still in it, I cried and cried. It felt so good to be there, in her space, especially when I re-read a lot of the warm and comforting words written about her in the condolence cards. I finally had a few hours to myself, and I felt so very warm inside, possibly because I was feeling a real deep connection with my mother. Maybe her spirit was surrounding me, and deep down it was a realisation that I should really treasure being there in her house and her space, as it might be for the last time ever.

While I had been at home in England with the children on holiday and with the building work going on, I hadn't really had any time to reflect. Now it was time. I hadn't allowed myself enough time for mourning. Even though I had so desperately wanted to reflect and think of her, it wasn't until that evening in her house that I allowed myself to spend time thinking about what had happened, thinking about my mum, trying to feel her and make a connection with the loss. Perhaps I had abused my true feelings by not spending any time on them, but that evening I made a big step in my acceptance of loss.

The days that followed were emotional and complex while my four siblings and I tried to agree on how to share my parents' belongings among the five of us. Families are rooted in old behavioural patterns that are used to mark each one's place within the family set up and to enable everyone to survive and function as children. These old patterns all reemerged when it came to sharing the assets. We all had our favourite belongings, and often a particular thing was wanted by more than one of us. It triggered confrontation and arguments, and with no parent to iron out any disagreement, as there always had been in the past, this was a difficult part of the whole process. It became clear that all these belongings were not simply material objects, but each carried meaning and often emotional value. I realise this more so now as I am writing this. My inherited items are very much loved in our house in England. They evoke memories and bring a little presence of my parents into the house. I can understand how families often fall apart during this process. My advice is to try not to be too greedy and to apply a "give and take" attitude in this matter. I am so grateful that we worked it out amicably in the end. It wasn't without friction, but it was a matter of give and take, and it worked. It showed that our parents had imprinted values of love, tolerance, and awareness of others upon us.

7

Grieving

After returning from Holland we spent a week in a Victorian train carriage in the Suffolk countryside, I really relaxed there and felt the stress rolling down my shoulders. The summer holidays were exhausting, and while the boys were home and the builders were in the house, I just didn't get any time to grieve. Perhaps if I hadn't had all that distraction going on in my life, things may have been more emotional and difficult. The situation was difficult and emotional for the wrong reasons.

Thinking back, I craved some me time to go for walks and have little cries and think about my mum. When the children finally did go back to school after their summer break, about two and a half months after she died, I did get a little "me" time. Quite often, I visited my local cathedral in Canterbury or a local church. I would light a candle for my mum and sometimes my dad and have a little cry, which relieved a little of my grief. I enjoyed being in places of prayer and quietness. It felt good to have a quiet few tears in a sacred place, usually followed by walking out into normal life, as if nothing had happened to me and moving on. Little moments of reflection like these made me cope with walking back into real life. I'm sure there were many more people walking down the high street having similar tough times of bereavement. Nobody has it written on their foreheads, though. It's just an invisible little cloud hanging above them, drifting in and out, and all we can do in life is to move on and go with the flow and live in the moment. Friends would give me hugs or little strokes down my arm, but really I felt fine. I was happy that she was released from her pain and that I was relieved of the emotional times of going back and forth to Holland and saying goodbye as if it was the last time every time I left her. It had been emotionally exhausting, and I don't think I could have managed that way of living for much longer.

It is natural to lose your mother at some stage in your life, and all being well, every "child" will have to go through this time of parental loss. I was lucky to have had this period of ten months with her, knowing that she was terminally ill, which gave us the chance to say goodbye over a long period of time. We knew and were able to prepare and shape our life together on this earth as it drew to an end. We very much tried to accept and embrace this final journey on earth in a positive way. I had cried with my mother about the fact that we would have to say goodbye and that she was going to die. She allowed me to do part of my grieving while she was alive. The fact that she was dying was talked about and there was a realisation while she was still alive that change was coming. She helped me prepare for this irreversible painful fact that life without her was definite.

I have seen friends who lost their parents through sudden death, and they didn't have to see their parents go through pain and illness, which, to be fair was difficult and soul-destroying at times. After their loss, they often went through feelings of shock, denial, numbness, and guilt. These are feelings I didn't have to deal with after losing my parents because I had many months to prepare for what was to come, during which time any possible emotional blockages were unblocked.

If I had been given the choice before my parents' illnesses and asked how I would want them to die, I would have probably gone for sudden death. However, now that I have lost them both to cancer, I wouldn't hesitate to choose the slow illness because we as a family had the opportunity to transform the "gifted time" into something meaningful. During that time, we prepared together for the moment of death.

As I am writing this, I am asking myself the very same question. I am also asking myself what my parents would have chosen. Would I want to die a slow death or make a quick exit? It's a difficult question, and I think my parents' gift to us children was the amazing courage and acceptance in their battle with terminal illness. They embraced their destiny. I will pass this gift on to my children if the situation ever arises. I learned so much during those months of living with terminal illness. If I ever have to deal with it myself, I will embrace it, although I probably wouldn't choose it.

In the first six months after my mother's death, I seemed to be coping pretty well, considering I had only just lost her. I was able to plan ahead and enjoy spending time at home, and even time away on holiday if I wished to do so. Having been through this emotionally difficult year made me realise that my life was now simple and straightforward. Sometimes it takes challenging times to appreciate the simple things in life.

Six months after her death, January arrived, and so did the flu. I was forced to stop the "keeping going," and apart from having to do the basics, which was still a lot with three boys, I was forced to just be. I felt so exhausted and tired, and I wanted to ring my mother for moral support, but I couldn't. It was a really trying time, and I really missed talking to her. For five weeks, I was incapable of doing much apart from lying down. Not only did I have the flu, but I believe I was totally burned out and in need of rest, just to be and grieve. I couldn't maintain any control of what was happening to me. I started missing my mum more and more. It was a harsh reality that I couldn't be in touch with her. Somehow during this time, I was finding tranquility within. I had no choice but to make myself aware of what I was experiencing inside. There were more bouts of grieving, which made me feel real emptiness inside. It's a feeling that anybody who has been bereaved will recognise, but it's a feeling that is hard to describe.

For me, it is like experiencing a void right in the middle of my solar plexus (in the middle of and bottom of your rib cage). It's like somebody has given you a mental punch just in that place, and you end up feeling really empty with a sense of nothingness in that spot. It hits you out of the blue, and suddenly there is a sense of no blood flowing, no moving muscles, no life existing, just a big empty hole with the rest of your body functioning normally and doing its usual thing around this empty space. When you get struck with a grieving moment, your mind goes off into a daydream, and nice memories and thoughts about the person who died take over, accompanied by tears welling up in your eyes and flowing down your cheeks. When your mind stagnates like this, it's a really comforting feeling because the person is so very much a part of your thinking. But at the same time, there is a sense of loss and realisation that you will never see that person again. Questions of death and the afterlife arise in your mind and conflict with the pleasing thoughts that you are experiencing. Every time you grieve, it's a bittersweet contrast, the feeling of deep love going hand in hand with the feeling of great loss.

I could switch these grieving moments on just like that. All I had to do was listen to some classical music or pick up a picture of her. These moments were important because they would provoke a release of emotion. Often, when I had time to myself, I would choose to have such a moment. It was like having a little bit of virtual time with my mother.

I would pick up a precancer picture of her in happier times. I felt that I had mourned her being ill and initially was happy for her to be released of her pain and suffering, but I now felt more bereft of what she used to be before she fell ill. It was also a realisation that mourning is very much done on your own. After six months, most people expect you to have moved on. Friends take less notice of your feelings, and there certainly aren't any more cards or flowers. However, the real pain and sense of loss often really occur around this time.

This is when we planted a Ghinko tree in her memory, just like we planted a tulip tree for my father a couple of months after his death. Having those trees gives me a little place to visit. Instead of visiting their graves, which are far away in Holland, I visit their individual trees.

I hope they will both grow into beautiful, healthy, big trees in the years to come, by which time I will probably have moved on.

The months leading up to the one-year anniversary of Mum's death were again difficult. I often revisited the moments that had happened a year before when she was still with us, when I could still see her and speak to her. It made me realise how much easier my life was a year on and that I wouldn't want to re visit those testing times again. I had not found it difficult to accept the fact that she died. We all have to let go of our parents at some stage in our lives, and I'm glad those difficult journeys in my life are behind me now.

Letting go is so much part of life. It starts at the moment the umbilical cord is cut, and it continues until we take our last breath. As I cycled my youngest son to nursery, days before the first anniversary of my mother's death, I realised that this was also soon coming to an end. Rufus was starting big school, and only a handful of cycling trips through the woods to nursery were left. I squeezed his perfect little hand, which was held by the hand of a mother who loves him unconditionally as we cycled through the tunnel of green beauty, knowing too well that another era was slowly fading away. The realisation of this imminent change brought me intense happiness in that perfect moment. This would soon become a fond memory. I would move on and accept and embrace the new times ahead. I knew that at the root of change would be growth. Change should not be resisted. It will take place no matter what. It is up to us if we choose to find the gifts hidden among the often chaotic times that change will bring.

Since losing my parents, I have become so much more aware that life should be lived just in the moment. Due to the difficult times we have had to go through as a family, I can now fully appreciate and realise what real happiness and joy are about. They are found in the simplest of things.

My uncle's funeral took place on the first anniversary of my mother's death. "If you lead a life of simplicity, life is simple." This is the quote that accompanied the photograph handed out at the service.

I wouldn't have understood this phrase when I entered my forties seven years ago, when I still had both parents and a successful and busy career, but I do now. The sadness of losing them, the intensity of living their last few months with them, and having to let go has, in return, brought me more joy in life. I look at myself and enjoy what I do have, and I don't covet what I don't. I have learned that true happiness is found in the small things. I have realised that life is too short for creating negative energy and that you can transform negative into positive by simple steps such as forgiveness, acceptance, and love.

On the day of the first anniversary of my mum's passing, I went to church for some reflection and prayer. In church, you are forced to stop and be. I enjoyed just sitting alone in a pew and thinking about my mother without any interruption while feeling at one with the congregation as we sang hymns and prayed for people living in pain and fear around the world.

I am delighted for my mother that her greatest fear of ending up demented in an old-peoples' home will never come true. I feel that she is still very much part of my life. I can sense her presence sometimes, and I strongly believe that she is around me. I know for sure that she is part of me. She has given me many values in life, and I thank her for that. Most of all, she has taught me how to be a good person by giving and spreading love around her little world. I believe this is the essence of life and happiness. At the end of the day, if you are loved and can give love, it should be the medicine for a good night's sleep.

The first anniversary of her death on June 30 came and went. I took a little time out and wrote a poem to her:

A year ago today
Your angels took you away.
I think about you every day,
And heal my loss in my own little way.
I make sure there are always flowers in your vase,

And when in need, I hold your picture in my hand and have a
little cry and
wonder where you've gone.
Away from me you travel to the highest light,
But in my heart you still live in full.

8

My Journey of Closure

SEPTEMBER 4, 2013
FOURTEEN MONTHS AFTER MY MOTHER'S DEATH
MY JOURNEY OF CLOSURE

It was the end of a long and sunny summer holidays and the day before Rufus's first day at school.

I had been feeling unusually low for the last couple of weeks during the summer break, but couldn't quite put my finger on it. The death of both my parents brought me face to face with my own mortality. The attention from friends was missing. Most of them were on holiday. Seeing a kind friend would have helped me deal with such issues that arise at these emotional times after losing both parents. It was also the first Summer holidays in my lifetime that I hadn't spent any time in Holland. My mother's house had been rented out, which meant that my physical base in Holland had now also been taken away from me. I wasn't able to call that house my home anymore. Strangers were living there now, and I just couldn't get myself to take on the difficult emotions that would await me when going to Holland. The next visit would have to be postponed until the autumn holidays. Trying to escape negative feelings by not going to Holland hadn't worked though as the reality of it was that I was still overshadowed with the same issues at home in England.

The harsh reality was that my unconditional love and my place I called home in Holland was now gone forever. There was no going back to be nurtured and loved by my dear parents anymore. Now that the house was rented out, there was not even the comfort of travelling back to their beautiful house and garden. The garden they were both so proud of, where we used to walk and talk about the flowers, where my mother would pick a beautiful bouquet that she would lovingly wrap in water for me to take back to England. It was the garden where I spent my last precious moments with my father, when we both subconsciously knew it was our last time together and we sat quietly, the day before he died, feeling such intense love for each other. Their garden was a sanctuary for me, where so many treasured memories had been created.

That evening of anticipation, I wanted to spend some extra time with Rufus at bedtime to prepare us for the big day coming up when I had to let go of my baby boy. We talked about what would be happening on his first day at school. While we were chatting quite happily, it suddenly hit me that my mum would be so proud and happy for him to start school. I was overcome by real sadness that she wouldn't be able to see him in his little school uniform. I asked Rufus if he thought Oma would be there with us the next day, meaning in spirit. He answered. "No, Oma won't be there. She is in heaven, Mummy!"

I said, "Perhaps she can see us from heaven?"

He replied. "No, Mummy. Oma can't see, but you can see her picture every day on the iPad if you want to!"

I felt overcome by sadness and overwhelmed with tears, and I experienced an intense physical hurt on my chest. My heart was aching for her. Rufus told me not to cry, but I told him that I was sad that Oma would not be there to see him go to school. I told him that Mummy needs to cry sometimes and that it's OK for mummies to be sad because tears often make you feel better. After those words, he still felt the need to do something to stop me crying and went to get the little musical box that my mum had given him a few weeks after she had been diagnosed with cancer. He opened the lid, and the familiar tune that came out reminded us of her. Rufus managed to include my mother in this precious time by his act, which resulted in more tears and release of the pain that I felt that evening. My mother had filled the box with precious little stones and a heart, which Rufus gently took out. We held the stones and talked about their beauty while the sound of the familiar and gentle tune filled his cosy little bedroom. An amber necklace, a first birthday gift to him from her that he used to wear daily, was also in the musical box. He took it out and gave it to me. He wanted me to wear it on his first day of school. He refused to close the box until I had stopped crying. I felt blessed to have such a beautiful and caring little boy to cherish. He was able to join ours and my mother's spirits in his unique little way.

SEPTEMBER 5, 2013

We woke up to a beautiful sunny day. It was the hottest September day in ten years. I was excited and apprehensive for Rufus and myself but admittedly also looking forward to having some time to myself again after four years of hard work and grief. It certainly felt as if a new chapter in my life was looming just around the corner.

Rufus did not object to his all new school uniform that morning and all went to plan. So far so good. We got to school in good time. Rufus kissed me goodbye and went in with his fellow pupils with no complications whatsoever. However, I was hiding my tears behind my sunglasses. The tears weren't for my little boy; they were for my parents. An emptiness and a great sense of loss engulfed me, and I was feeling hurt in my heart. I was craving the love of my parents and felt deprived of them not being part of my life anymore. All I wanted that day was to be able to pick up the phone and share with them about Rufus starting school. That was all!

I chose to be positive, though, and walk the two miles home from school through the footpaths, picking blackberries on my way. A good friend who also dropped her youngest boy off for his first day at school joined me on the first half of my walk. She is a good listener, and I was grateful her being there with me. We both contemplated what was to come and reflected on what had been. We were both on the brink of a new phase and declared our friendship for each other. I felt blessed for having her in my life, and after saying goodbye to her, I continued my walk across the glorious and sunny Kent countryside that would lead me home.

I paused my walk to pick blackberries in the hot sunshine. A strong sense of calm came over me. The sounds of nature became richer. The simplicity of the gathering of fruit gave me the opportunity to feel at peace with the sounds of the sheep in the surrounding fields and with the birds hidden among the greenery around me. Their tunes sounded effortless and filled with joy on that memorable September morning. In the distance, I could hear some dogs barking and lorries reversing, but in my mind they were far away from this tranquil moment. I felt a deep presence of my new life that was emerging. I chose to stay in this moment until I had gathered a wholesome little crop of blackberries. As I walked on, I met a local farmer and had a little chat about the gorgeous weather we had been having and shared a little village gossip. I didn't feel rushed at all and enjoyed just being in my familiar patch of land on my first day of freedom in a long time. I was at liberty to do what I wanted to do. This was a day I had been looking forward to.

I proceeded on my walk until I came to a gate that stopped me in my tracks. I didn't want to open it. I looked over the gate, and the view was familiar. I had opened this gate many times in the past, but today was different. This gate was symbolising something. I thought that perhaps it was a figuration of an entrance to a new phase of my life. I hung over the gate and cried. Tears were being released from my eyes, and I allowed it to happen while I was looking at the tranquil scenery that lay beyond that gate. A white butterfly appeared near me, which added to the beauty of the view. I remembered that my mum had said, only a few days before she died, that if she were to come back, it would be as a butterfly. I thought that perhaps it was a sign but not strong enough for me to open the gate. I continued to stand there and cry, reflect, and feel an emptiness that was significant at that moment of time in my life. I was overwhelmed by the power that this metaphoric moment had on me, and I chose to be aware of it and experience the intensity of these feelings of loss, the absence of loved ones, and the unknown that lay ahead.

Before I opened the gate, I wanted to look back to see where I had walked from. When I turned around, I realised that I had just walked from a dead field. The grass on the land had dried out during the hot summer and looked lifeless. Beyond the grass field were green trees. The earth I had just walked from was symbolising the previous four years, which had been overpowered by grief and death. Rufus had been our new life that had pulled us through this dark period, and today I had to let go of him as he started a new phase in his life—and so would I. While I stood there looking over the dead brown field, the little white butterfly flew across the gate to be in the dead field with me. This time, I knew it was a sign from my mother. I was so moved that it had come to find me in the field that I was now facing. As I was drawn in by it, the butterfly flew back over the gate, leading me to open it and walk into the next chapter of my live. It made me realise that I needed to not hold back but rather open my heart fully for the happiness that I would find beyond that gate. My mother was guiding me. With that knowledge, I merrily opened the gate to a new era. I learned on that very day that I will always be guided home by loving angels of this world and of the spiritual world, just like my parents were guided home by their angels on their journeys home.

You can find some pictures which were taken during Dianne's journey in "Given Time to Say Goodbye" on her website.
www.losingaparenttocancer.com

www.facebook.com/GivenTimetoSayGoodbye

Review the book if you like it!

Resources that may help you cope with loss and grief

<u>Help with cancer (UK)</u>

http://www.macmillan.org.uk

http://www.canceradvice.co.uk/support-groups/

<u>Help with bereavement</u>

http://www.cruse.org.uk

http://www.bereavementadvice.org

http://www.childbereavementuk.org

http://www.bereavementcharity.org.uk

http://www.bereavement.co.uk

http://www.merrywidow.me.uk

<u>Help with bereavement by suicide or feeling suicidal</u>

http://www.sobs.admin.care4free.net

http://www.samaritans.org

<u>Dealing with death and terminal illness (further afield)</u>

http://www.ekrfoundation.org

http://healgrief.org

http://www.nhpco.org

http://www.opentohope.com

http://thegrieftoolbox.com

http://www.thewhpca.org

About the Author

Dianne Leutner, a Dutch national who now lives in England, knows the depths of grief firsthand after losing both her parents to terminal cancer and two sisters-in-law to sudden death within just a few years. It's no surprise, then, that her first two books focus on the topic of loss.

Her debut book, *Remembering*, is a children's bereavement book that was nominated at the BMA 2010 Book Awards, remains one of Child Bereavement UK's best-selling books, and is heralded by the British Medical Association.

For fifteen years, Leutner worked in TV and radio production as a script supervisor, director, and producer. The author is passionate about helping others learn how to grieve well so they, too, can fully embrace life.

46926967R00125

Printed in Poland
by Amazon Fulfillment
Poland Sp. z o.o., Wrocław